MILE MARKERS OF

FAITH

DAVID L. SLATER

ISBN 978-1-0980-6983-4 (paperback)
ISBN 978-1-0980-6984-1 (digital)

Christian Faith Publishing, Inc.
832 Park Avenue
Meadville, PA 16335
www.christianfaithpublishing.com

Scriptures marked NIV are taken from the NEW INTERNATIONAL VERSION (NIV): Scripture taken from THE HOLY BIBLE, NEW INTERNATIONAL VERSION ®. Copyright© 1973, 1978, 1984, 2011 by Biblica, Inc.™. Used by permission of Zondervan.

Scriptures marked NAS are taken from the NEW AMERICAN STANDARD (NASB): Scripture taken from the NEW AMERICAN STANDARD BIBLE®, copyright© 1960, 1962, 1963, 1968, 1971, 1972, 1973, 1975, 1977, 1995 by The Lockman Foundation. Used by permission.

Printed in the United States of America

INTRODUCTION

I love to drive! There is a sense of freedom and serenity in heading down the open road, passing through beautiful country as you move from a starting point toward your final destination. Along most roads you travel, you will notice mile markers that, depending on your direction of travel, either count up or down each mile of progress on your journey. While the ultimate goal is your final destination, perhaps hundreds or even thousands of miles away, these mile markers provide shorter goals that help break the trip up into more manageable legs. A short-term goal may be to count down the miles to the next town to stop for gas and get a bite to eat, or when to stop for the night, find a motel room, and get a good night's sleep before rising early in the morning to begin the next leg of the trip.

In a similar sense, the same is true where "the rubber meets the road" on our journey of faith in Jesus Christ. Our final destination is our home in heaven to be with Christ, but many miles must be travelled through life in this world before we reach our ultimate goal. Just as mile markers break up our road trips, so the Scriptures provide us with spiritual mile markers that help break our journey of faith into more manageable goals and also gauge our progress in faith along the way.

In my personal journey of faith, I have found the New Testament Epistle of James a great source of invaluable mile markers. James isn't theoretical. He doesn't engage in deep theological discussions. Rather, he focuses on our immediate needs and common problems and shows us how to apply our faith in Jesus Christ to our daily experiences.

It is my prayer this devotional helps you on your journey of faith to a fuller enjoyment of Christian liberty, a greater peace, and the absolute confidence of your safe arrival at our final destination: the home in heaven Jesus, according to His promise in John 14:1–3, is preparing for all those who have trusted Him as their Lord and Savior.

> Do not let your heart be troubled; believe in God, believe also in Me. In My Father's house are many dwelling places; if it were not so, I would have told you; for I go to prepare a place for you. If I go and prepare a place for you, I will come again and receive you to Myself, that where I am, *there* you may be also. (John 14:1–3)

LIVING IN THE SHADOWS

I t's a near-perfect midsummer day. It's a balmy seventy-five degrees with a light breeze and low humidity. The sun is shining, and its warmth feels good on your face as you're cruising down the road with your convertible top down. Seemingly out of nowhere, a large dark cloud comes blowing over a hill; and as it drifts over the sun, a shadow races across the ground toward you. It passes over and engulfs you in its gloom and immediately robs you of the warmth of the sun on your face; you feel a chill go down your back, and goose bumps begin to form on your skin.

If you've ever had that experience, then you have at least a small idea of how it feels for many people who live in the shadows. It may be in the shadow of an older sibling or more popular friends, or watching first-string team members from the bench, or feeling left in the dust by a hard-charging peer at work. Whatever the circumstance, living in the shadow of another can be lonely and damaging to a person's self-worth and even make one angry and resentful.

James was Jesus's younger half brother. Jesus was, of course, the Son of God conceived by the Holy Spirit in the Virgin Mary, and James was a natural-born son of Joseph and Mary; so James grew up with Jesus. Think of how hard it must've been for James to grow up in the shadow of an older brother who never sinned, never misbehaved, and always obeyed His parents. Jesus was literally the perfect son.

I can hear Joseph and Mary scolding poor James. "Why can't you be more like your brother Jesus?" Like many middle children, James probably felt like Jesus was Mom and Dad's favorite to whom he could never measure up no matter how hard he tried. As a matter of fact, the Bible makes it clear that James was envious of Jesus and resented Him.

The only time Jesus's brothers, for He had more than one, are mentioned in the Gospels, the circumstances are less than friendly. Mark 3:20–21(NASB) says of Jesus, "And He came home, and the crowd gathered again, to such an extent that they could not even eat a meal. When His own people heard *of this*, they went out to take custody of Him; for they were saying, 'He has lost His senses,'" The word translated as "people" is the Greek word for "kinsmen," "His kin," "His family," which is exactly how the New International Version (NIV) translates it. In Mark 3:31, this meaning is confirmed when they are specifically identified as Jesus's "mother and his brothers." So as Jesus is presenting Himself to the nation as the Son of God and the promised Messiah by preaching and working miracles, his family tries to get Jesus to cool it, come home, and stop embarrassing them with all His God talk, even to the point of suggesting to the crowd that He was out of His mind. "Hey, don't listen to Jesus. He's been out in the sun too long and is touched in the head."

On another occasion, envious of Jesus's popularity with the crowds, His brothers falsely accuse Him of wanting to go to Jerusalem during the time of the Passover feast just so He could be seen and become more famous.

> After these things Jesus was walking in Galilee,
> for He was unwilling to walk in Judea because

the Jews were seeking to kill Him. Now the feast of the Jews, the Feast of Booths, was near. Therefore, His brothers said to Him, "Leave here and go into Judea, so that Your disciples also may see Your works which You are doing. For no one does anything in secret when he himself seeks to be *known* publicly. If You do these things, show Yourself to the world." For not even His brothers were believing in Him. (John 7:1–5 NASB)

None of Jesus's brothers, James included, believed in Him as the Son of God, acknowledged Him as "the Christ," and trusted Him as Lord and Savior.

However, all that changed for James after Jesus rose from the dead. First Corinthians 15:4–7 records that after His resurrection, Jesus appeared to Cephas (Peter), the eleven disciples together, and a crowd of about five hundred of His followers; and then He singled out James for a one-on-one encounter. We can only imagine how James might have responded to seeing his brother crucified and die now alive and well, but I seriously doubt he would've sarcastically responded with "Hey, dead brother, how's it hanging? Oh, sorry, poor choice of words."

Quite the contrary, I have no doubt James fell to his knees in fear and amazement and trusted Jesus as His Lord and Savior. How could you say, "No," to an offer of forgiveness and eternal life from the risen Lord Himself?

Talk about a mile marker, James's encounter with the resurrected Lord marked not just a point on his journey but a completely new direction and destination for his life. He was a changed man! James would no longer live jealously in the shadow of Jesus as his older brother but in the light of Jesus as his Lord and Savior.

James squandered much of his early life as an unbeliever; even watching Jesus's three years of earthly ministry teaching God's truth and working incredible miracles, he remained on the sidelines mostly feeling indifference toward Jesus and even hostility at times. But it is never too late to be saved, and there is nothing Jesus cannot forgive.

If you have been indifferent or even hostile toward Jesus but now see Him as the risen Lord and Savior He is, I invite you to trust Him. Right now in the quietness of your thoughts, pray to God and tell Him you believe that Jesus Christ was God in the flesh Who died, was buried, and rose again to pay the price for your sins. Ask Him to forgive you, wash away all your sins, and give you eternal life.

> Draw near to God and he will draw near to you.
> (James 4:8)

A NEW DIRECTION

(JAMES 1:1)

I doubt that any of us with much driving experience have not made a wrong turn and had to "flip a U-ey" to head in the right direction. Well, what is true of driving can also be true in life. Whether by developing a bad habit, or making a serious error in judgment, or falling into sin because we started running with the wrong crowd, sometimes we need to "flip a U-ey" in order to change the direction of our life. The Bible calls that "repentance." There can be no repentance without first admitting that we are wrong, that our life is headed in the wrong direction, and that we are willing to make a 180-degree turn in the right direction.

James began his life living in Jesus's shadow. As any of us would, he resented the rebukes of his parents to be more like his literally perfect older brother. He was envious of Jesus's rising popularity with the crowds who flocked to Him to see His miracles and hear His teaching. James didn't want to be compared with Jesus, or known only as "Jesus's little brother." No, he wanted to be his own man, be known for his own successes, and make his own unique mark in the world, until, of course, he met the risen Lord.

As soon as James stopped seeing Jesus as just his older brother and accepted Him as his Lord and Savior, all selfish desire for personal recognition and a life of his own was replaced with a new desire to proclaim the name of Jesus. Though he could have boasted of being the half brother of Jesus, he chose instead to introduce himself in his epistle as "James, a bond-servant of God and of the Lord Jesus Christ" (James 1:1).

The word *bond-servant* is the Greek word used of a person who voluntarily submitted himself to another to be their permanent slave. James only wanted to be known as someone who had laid everything he was and everything he had at the feet of Jesus to be His servant for the rest of his life. Talk about a change in direction! All his desire to assert self and live for himself was replaced with a passion to live for Jesus.

Who and what do you live for? If life is mostly just about you and what makes you happy, then you're headed in the wrong direction. If you claim Jesus to be your Lord and Savior, let me ask you: do you have the desire to willingly be a bond-servant of Jesus Christ, or would you have to admit that though you have received His forgiveness and eternal life, you've done very little to really serve Him as your Lord? Perhaps it's time to "flip a U-ey" and put the Lord Jesus first.

> For am I now seeking the favor of men, or of God?
> Or am I striving to please men? If I were still trying to please men, I would not be a bond-servant
> of Christ. (Galatians 1:10)

TRAVELING COMPANIONS

(JAMES 1:1)

As many men in their forties do, I guess I went through my "mid-life crisis" and bought a Harley. As a Navy chaplain serving with a Marine infantry battalion, I had just returned from my second deployment to Iraq and was looking forward to the freedom of the open road with my wife, Tracie, behind me and her arms wrapped around me. It turned out that she didn't really enjoy riding as much as I did, so I ended up making most of my rides alone.

Over the next several years, I rode less and less until finally I realized I hadn't ridden the Harley more than once or twice in the last year, so I ended up selling it. The fact is that it just wasn't that much fun riding alone without my wife. Though I truly enjoy the freedom of the open road, leaning through the turns with the wind in my face, it could never satisfy my deeper longing for someone to share the journey with me.

I guess that's why I relate so much to James. Once he accepted Christ as his Lord, he held on to the idea that his faith was not some private thing he should keep to himself but something to be experienced and shared with others. He writes his letter "to the twelve tribes who are dispersed abroad" (James 1:1) in order to share his faith and knowledge of God with his fellow Jewish citizens scattered all over the known world and, by extension, across time to us today.

As you read through James's letter, you will notice that he often refers to his readers as "brethren," "my brethren," "my beloved brethren." Fifteen times he uses these words of kinship and companionship toward us as his siblings in Christ. He recognized that we are on this journey together and need each other as brothers and sisters in the family of God.

Though I like to think of myself as a strong, independent person, and I think most of us do, the truth is that we need companionship. After God created Adam, He said, "It is not good for man to be alone; I will make him a helper suitable for him" (Genesis 2:18). God made us to need and share our lives with others. For most of us, God's plan is for us to find that "special someone" to marry and raise a family with, but whether married or single, we all need some special traveling companions on the road of life. Whether a beloved sibling or a best friend, God says we need other people to accompany us on life's journey.

We cannot live out our faith in God alone. It has to be lived out with others and for others, which is why God ordained the church. Let's be honest: if you have ever gone through a season of life when you stopped going to church, it is almost certain you also slid backward in your relationship with God and in the practice of your faith. What more proof do you need? Stop trying to navigate your faith alone! Join a good church where God's Word is treasured and taught; get plugged back into the body of Christ and share the journey with your brothers and sisters.

Let us hold fast the confession of our hope without wavering, for He who promised is faithful; and let us consider how to stimulate one another to love and good deeds, not forsaking our own assembling together, as is the habit of some, but encouraging one another; and all the more as you see the day drawing near. (Hebrews 10:23–25)

CONSTRUCTION ZONE FIVE MILES AHEAD

(JAMES 1:2)

Several years back on a family vacation with my wife and two young children, we were rolling down the interstate in Colorado when those most dreaded words loomed on a yellow sign on the side of the road: "Construction Zone Five Miles Ahead. Be prepared to stop." Well, I wasn't prepared to stop! You see, when I travel, I'm on a schedule. I plan to cover so many miles a day to arrive at my destination in as few days as possible. Construction zones and traffic jams just weren't part of the plan, but planned or not, in about two miles, all westbound traffic came to a complete stop, which meant the interstate was backed up three miles from whatever caused the stoppage.

I came to find out later that they were blasting rock off the mountain on the north side of the highway, and traffic had to be stopped not just for the detonation but for as long as it took to clear the fallen rock off the road. So there we sat for about an hour and a half, making no progress. No mile markers were flying by, and it was clear we were not going to make it to the town I had made my goal to stop at for the night. Well, let me tell you: even if it had been Christmas, this traveler would not have been singing "Joy to the World." The sad truth is that joy was the last thing on my mind, and every attempt of my sweet, patient wife to help me think otherwise was not going to change my bad attitude one bit.

Though many years later, I must confess that I still tend toward impatience on the road, but some godly advice from James has helped me tremendously. James 1:2 says, "Consider it all joy, my brethren, when you encounter various trials." God says that our first reaction to trials should be one of joy. Now, that's the exact opposite of our natural, knee-jerk reaction to troubles, isn't it? But that's the point. As Christians, our reaction to trials should be better than the natural, knee-jerk reaction of most other people. So what can we do to prepare ourselves to react differently?

First of all, expect that trials will come. The word *various* in James 1:2 carries the idea that trials come in many shapes, sizes, and shades of intensity. Some are relatively minor annoyances, and some are major tragedies. Some are generic to all of us, and some are intensely personal. Sometimes trials come one at a time, and sometimes "when it rains, it pours."

James says we should expect that any and all of these could happen at any time. Notice he used the word *when*, not *if*, so that in expecting trials, we wouldn't be caught off guard. Stuff happens to all of us. It's part of the human condition for believers and unbelievers alike, so the more we expect them, the more prepared we will be to handle them without losing our minds or our joy.

I like what 1 Peter 4:12 says: "Beloved, do not be surprised at the fiery ordeal among you, which comes upon you for your testing, as though some strange thing were happening to you; but to the degree that you share the sufferings of Christ keep on rejoicing, so that also at the revelation of His glory you may rejoice with exultation." The point is that, whether because of our humanity or our faith, we should all expect trials!

Second, when trials do come, think before you act. James says, "Consider it all joy." Knee-jerk reactions come from our emotions, but intelligent, rational, thoughtful reactions come from a mind that considers the facts and weighs them properly.

We all know from experience that trials are not joyful experiences. God is not suggesting that we just laugh our way through troubles, joke about them, and try not to take them seriously. That's just a form of denial that clouds good judgment. Rather, by the word *consider*, God is telling us that our response to trials and troubles must be to think it through, to ask ourselves, "Is this really a big deal?"

I don't know about you, but I tend to handle big trials pretty well. Sickness, an accident, even the death of a loved one I accept as part of life in a sinful, fallen world, and I trust God to guide me through it; and He has always supplied His "grace to help" in my time of need (Hebrews 4:16).

But on "one of those days" when I bend over to tie my shoe and the lace breaks, and I get ready to go to work and my tire is flat, and now I'm running late, and don't you know it, I get stuck behind some granny doing thirty-five in a fifty-five zone—aaaahh!

Ever been there? Think with your head now, not your heart. Are any of these things, even taken altogether, really that big a deal? Nobody has died. The sky is not falling. It's not the end of the world. Is it really worth the high blood pressure, maybe cussing out poor granny and making a reckless attempt to pass when it's not really safe? Yes, I'm ashamed to say I have done all of the above.

When you really think about it, doesn't it seem foolish to get so upset? Hasn't God promised to supply His "grace to help in time of need" with these kinds of problems too?

Emotions cause knee-jerk reactions. They make "mountains out of molehills." They make relatively minor irritations seem like the end of the world. They make us lose our joy, if not our minds altogether. Emotions alone only cloud our judgment, so we can't see the trial clearly and respond properly; so God says think about it, put it in perspective, and make an intelligent appraisal of your situation.

Again, Peter echoes James in 1 Peter 5:7: "Cast all your anxiety on Him because He cares for you." Bring all your trials and troubles, big or small, to God, and you won't lose your joy.

STOP AND SMELL
THE ROSES

(JAMES 1:3–4)

So there we were, stopped on the interstate, going nowhere for about an hour and a half. I was foolishly fuming at the delay, but my wife and kids saw it as a wonderful opportunity to "stop and smell the roses." It was a beautiful, warm, sunny day. The mountain scenery, so easily missed when speeding by at seventy miles per hour, was absolutely breathtaking to just stand there and take in.

It took a while, but as I watched my wife enjoying the warmth of the sun on her face and saw the wind blow through her beautiful hair and my kids having a ball running around and playing, I at least started to realize the delay wasn't important enough to ruin their fun with my bad attitude. My son, who loved to collect rocks, even got a chance to explore along the road and find some interesting rocks to add to his collection. To me, the delay was still a bother and a hindrance to my travel plans; but to them, it was an adventure to take advantage of and enjoy. Even then, and more so today, I envy their ability to recognize the good in what may at first seem like a bad situation.

When considering any kind of trial, James 1:3–4 says we must remember "that the testing of your faith produces endurance. And let endurance have *its* perfect result, so that you may be perfect and complete, lacking in nothing." In other words, we need to recognize the good that can come from our troubles—how it can help us learn patience, build endurance, become more flexible, and grow to maturity.

Just as the trials of physical exercise strengthen our muscles and cardiovascular system to improve our physical endurance, life's trials strengthen our faith and improve our spiritual endurance. Why do we put ourselves through all the sweat and pain of a workout? Because we recognize the good! We can smile and say, "No pain, no gain," because we know we'll look better, feel better, and enjoy long-term health benefits for staying in shape. Recognizing the good is what helps us gut it out.

Yet when the trials of life and faith hit us, what tends to be our first question? "God, why?" Well, this answers the question, doesn't it? God allows us to experience trials to stretch, strengthen, and test our faith to buff up our spiritual muscles. Maybe we all can't have six-pack abs, but we can have six-pack faith, but not without trials to make our faith perfect and complete.

The word *perfect* does not mean faultless but refers to something fully grown or mature. The idea is that without trials, we would never fully develop our character or grow to maturity in attitude or faith. We would just stay spiritual babies. The word *complete* adds the idea of being whole, of something that has all its parts. Even a mature Christian can be lacking in certain areas of life or character and still need trials to make them the whole, well-rounded Christian God desires all of us to be.

God says in Ephesians 4 that He desires all of His children to become mature "to the measure of the stature which belongs to the fullness of Christ" (verse 13), and we are to "grow up in all aspects into Him who is the head, even Christ" (verse 15).

When trials come, big or little, one at a time or a truckload all at once, it helps to know and recognize in advance the good purpose God has in our pain. He uses it to make us more like Christ. "Well," you might say, "that sounds nice, but it doesn't make the pain of suffering any less." No, it doesn't, but knowing God's reason and purpose for our pain does help us see value in our suffering and endure it more patiently.

> And not only this, but we also exult in our tribulations, knowing that tribulation brings about perseverance; and perseverance, proven character; and proven character, hope; and hope does not disappoint, because the love of God has been poured out within our hearts through the Holy Spirit who was given to us. (Romans 5:3–5)

ASK FOR DIRECTIONS

(JAMES 1:5)

Okay, I get it. When trouble comes, I'm supposed to rejoice by recognizing the good that God can do through my suffering to make me more like Christ. But what if I can't see the good? What if there doesn't seem to be any "silver lining in the dark cloud," and I can't imagine any way forward where good could ever come from this pain? James 1:5 advises us to ask for directions. "But if any of you lacks wisdom, let him ask of God, who gives to all generously and without reproach, and it will be given to him."

As a man, and I think I speak for most men, I hate to ask for directions. I'm not about to admit to some other guy that I'm lost and don't know how to get to where I'm going! Forget that. All I need is a map, and if a map is not available, I'll figure it out for myself anyway.

Perhaps it's less of an issue today than it used to be. It doesn't hurt our pride to admit ignorance to our car's navigation system or a GPS app on our phone, so we'll not only ask them for directions when we're lost but rely on them to get us around on almost a daily basis.

Well, if it doesn't hurt our pride to ask GPS for directions to reach a desired destination, why would we hesitate to ask our all-knowing God for directions on which way to turn in life? Let's face it: none of us are perfect and complete in our faith. Therefore, it stands to reason we won't understand every trial that comes or know which way to go in response to it, so ask God. God says it's okay to ask. He won't scold us for asking and instead promises to generously give us the wisdom we seek.

It may be that the very purpose God intends our trial to accomplish is simply to lift our thoughts and hearts to Him. God always wants our hearts raised heavenward, so when trials come and you can't see the hand of God at work, raise your heart heavenward and ask for wisdom. God says it's okay to ask. He won't scold you for asking. He will generously give you the wisdom you seek.

But here's the thing: we have to ask the right question. Don't ask God, "Why?" That's the wrong question. Quite frankly, God does not have to explain Himself to us or justify His actions to us by telling us why. He is our infinitely loving, good, and just God Who deserves our absolute trust. What we should ask God is, "What now? God, what would You have me learn from this trial? What would You have me do in response to it? Where do I go from here?"

Knowing "why" really changes nothing. It accomplishes nothing. Nor does it give us any direction on what to do next. However, knowing "what now" changes everything because it gives us direction and purpose to move forward with God's help. If you are hurting and your prayers for wisdom have gone unanswered, perhaps it's because you have been asking the wrong question. Stop asking God why He allowed the trial and ask Him for directions instead.

Trials are a pain, literally! Nobody likes them, and nobody wants them. But the truth is we all need them to grow and mature in character and faith. Let's be honest: when are we most likely to turn to God, pray more fervently, and search the Scriptures for wisdom? Is it when things are going great or when we are suffering through a trial of some kind? Sometimes it's only through pain that we are truly humbled enough to roll down the window of our pride and ask God for directions.

> Let him ask of God, who gives to all generously and without reproach, and it will be given to him. (James 1:5)

DETOURS OF DOUBT

(JAMES 1:6)

Many years ago, I was on a trip in very unfamiliar territory, so I had mapped out my route and written down directions I thought would get me directly to my desired destination. The trip was going just according to plan when I rolled up on a construction sign that said, "Detour Ahead." I hate detours! Not only do they usually cost more time, but they take me off the route I carefully planned and force me on an alternate route that I'm no longer sure will get me back to where I need to go. On my planned route, I'm confident I know exactly where I am and how I would get to where I'm going. However, now that I'm detoured, I have doubts. How far out of the way is this going to take me? How much time will I lose? Will the detour be clearly marked, or will I miss a turn and end up completely lost?

Normally, none of those worries are justified. Most of the time, the detours are clearly marked and get us quickly back where we are supposed to be, but this time, the detour took me miles out of the way on back roads full of twists and turns, and sure enough, somehow I missed one and ended up lost. No, I did not stop and ask for directions! Yes, I eventually found my way back to the main road I needed to be on. However, because of this bad experience, even though GPS has made detours much less worrisome, they still tend to take me out of my comfort zone and fill me with doubts about exactly where I am and where I need to be.

Ironically, when it comes to our journey of faith, it isn't so much a detour in some plan for life that causes us doubt. It is our doubts themselves that become the detour that leads us away from the most direct route of God's will for our lives. Doubts only create uncertainty, which causes us to question God's will or even resist obeying His will.

Doubt is the opposite of faith. The more we doubt God, whether it is His ability, goodness, love, plan for our life, or willingness to help, the less we will trust Him. Faith chases away doubt. The more we trust God, the less we will ever doubt Him. The less you doubt God, the more you will trust Him. It's as simple as that. Doubt negates faith. Faith chases away doubt. Ephesians 2:8–9 makes it clear that we can only be saved by grace through faith, not by works, and Hebrews 11:6 says, "Without faith it is impossible to please God." This is reason enough why doubt is so dangerous, because we can't come to God any other way but by faith. Doubt keeps us from God, but faith draws us near.

This is why James 1:6 says that whenever we ask God for wisdom, we must "ask in faith without any doubting," and goes on to warn us that doubt paralyzes us with indecision. The image of the "surf of the sea driven and tossed by the wind" is a perfect illustration for a person full of doubts. Just like the churning waves of the sea, the doubter is in a constant state of agitation, up and down, back and forth about which way to go and what to do next. They can't decide because they are driven by the winds of so many outside influences.

Faith always drives us in one direction: toward God, His Word, and His will for our lives, where we will always find grace and help in trials. Doubt drives us in every other direction. Because the doubter lacks the faith to stay focused on God, he is pulled between the forces of his circumstances, emotions, and conflicting advice of others.

Living with doubts about God is like being a rat lost in a maze scurrying back and forth in and out of dead ends, looking for a way out but not finding it. It's like floating in a raft in choppy seas, drifting with the swirling winds. Who knows where you'll end up?

If you find yourself agitated and cannot make up your mind how you should feel or what you should do, then you are probably struggling with doubts about God. God is not the author of confusion. God gives us clarity, confidence, joy, and a peace that passes all understanding. Pray; confess your doubts and ask God to calm your troubled waters.

> Be anxious for nothing, but in everything by prayer and supplication with thanksgiving let your requests be made known to God. And the peace of God, which surpasses all comprehension, will guard your hearts and your minds in Christ Jesus. (Philippians 4:6–7)

PRAYER FOR THE JOURNEY

(JAMES 1:6–7)

I was privileged to have Christian parents who loved the Lord and sought to model faith in Christ at home as well as on Sundays. Even from my earliest childhood days, I remember bowing in prayer in the car before we would begin a family trip or vacation to trust God for safe travel. *Trust* is the operative word! It would seem quite useless to bother to pray if we had any doubts God would hear or answer our prayer.

As we've already seen, any journey has the potential for things to go wrong, and the journey of life is no exception. Stuff happens, and when it does, we need to pray for wisdom. But when we do pray, James sternly warns us to pray "without any doubting...for that man ought not to expect that he will receive anything from the Lord"

(James 1:6–8). It may seem harsh, but God is not obligated to answer the prayers of doubting people.

Think about it this way. If a friend came to you all agitated about a problem, wanting assistance or advice, and said, "Hey, I doubt you can really help me, and if I don't like the sound of your advice, I probably won't listen and do what you suggest," and you know from experience this person has ignored your attempts to help before, how inclined would you be to waste your breath again? It may be that the best thing you can do for that person is to just let them learn the hard way.

Well, even more so, don't you think that God knows when He's wasting His breath? Doubters don't tend to listen very well. Instead of going to one trusted person and accepting their good advice, they will ask multiple people and then vacillate between all the different opinions. Doubters rarely make good decisions and stay the course to finish what they started. Their own doubts prevent them from receiving the very help they seek.

God expects and condescends to the doubts of unbelievers who are seeking to know Him. Of course they have doubts. They haven't believed and trusted Christ yet. But God expects more from His children. Isn't that also how we are? We can't expect or blame someone else's kid for doubting us or not trusting us. They're not our kid! But we do expect our own kids to know us well enough to trust us and not question our love or willingness to help them in a time of need.

James mentions another way that doubt hinders our prayers. The very idea of asking God to meet a need requires that we know what we should ask for, but the doubter isn't sure. Rather than praying with purpose, because the doubter is "double-minded," he has no clear sense of purpose to his prayers other than to escape the pain of the trial. Unfortunately, this is contrary to the will of God, who always has a purpose for the trials He allows into our lives.

This word translated as "double-minded" literally means "double-souled." It describes people who have no keen sense of direction in life, no clear sense of purpose, because their doubt causes them to constantly hesitate between two ways of thinking. One soul says, "I believe," while the other whispers, "I'm not sure." There is a divided allegiance that keeps the doubter from single-heartedly committing to God, so the doubting believer becomes "unstable in all his ways."

In every area of life, doubters never have a clear sense of purpose because they're always looking in two directions at the same time and arguing with themselves which one they should take. Torn between two worlds, they drift through life, taking it as it comes, sometimes choosing God and other times not, but always with a degree of uncertainty when they do and guilt when they don't. What an unsettled, frustrating, and sad way to live. Doubt is the antithesis of faith and has no place in the life and prayers of God's children. A doubting believer is an oxymoron, a contradiction of terms, and should not expect to "receive anything from the Lord."

> Such confidence we have through Christ toward God. Not that we are adequate in ourselves to consider anything as *coming* from ourselves, but our adequacy is from God, who also made us adequate *as* servants of a new covenant, not of the letter but of the Spirit; for the letter kills, but the Spirit gives life. (2 Corinthians 3:4–6)

BEWARE OF BLIND SPOTS

(JAMES 1:9–12)

No matter how well designed it may be, every car has its blind spots, those areas that the rear- and side-view mirrors can't completely cover. It is amazing how narrow pillars on either side of the rear window can momentarily hide even a large truck from view and potentially cause an accident. Many cars now have accident avoidance systems that sound a warning buzzer if a driver tries to change lanes when another car is hidden in a blind spot, and these warning systems have no doubt prevented many accidents.

Like all cars, all of us have blind spots too. We all have flaws and weaknesses of character that blind us to the dangers around us and lead to bad decisions that can wreck our lives and damage our faith. God says that doubt is one of those blind spots because the doubt we have during trials blinds us from seeing God's blessings.

James uses poverty and riches to illustrate how doubting God can so cloud our judgment that we can no longer see the blessings we still have in trials or the new blessings that come from our trials. James 1:9–12 says,

> But the brother of humble circumstances is to glory in his high position; and the rich man *is to glory* in his humiliation, because like flowering grass he will pass away. For the sun rises with a scorching wind and withers the grass; and its flower falls off and the beauty of its appearance is destroyed; so too the rich man in the midst of his pursuits will fade away. Blessed is a man who perseveres under trial; for once he has been approved, he will receive the crown of life which *the Lord* has promised to those who love Him.

From our perspective, we might say that poverty is a trial, but God says that poverty can be a blessing. Yes, poor Christians might be lacking in material goods, but they can also glory in the fact that they have fewer things to tie their hearts down to this world and fewer temptations to trust in riches rather than trust in God. Jesus said,

> Do not store up for yourselves treasures on earth, where moth and rust destroy, and where thieves break in and steal. But store up for yourselves treasures in heaven, where neither moth nor rust destroys, and where thieves do not break in or steal; for where your treasure is, there your heart will be also. (Matthew 6:19–20)

It's not a curse to be poor in worldly goods if it helps you become exceedingly rich in Christ, which is the greatest blessing of all. The truth is that being rich can be, and often is, a curse. It is much harder for rich Christians to trust God for daily needs than to trust in themselves. It is much harder for them to keep their hearts focused on Christ than on their investments and luxurious lifestyle. It would be a much harder trial for rich Christians to lose their wealth and end up poor than for a poor Christian who never knew wealth to be poor. Jesus also said in Matthew 19:24, "It is easier for a camel to pass through the eye of a needle than for a rich man to enter the kingdom of heaven," so wealth isn't necessarily the blessing it seems. It is certainly a curse for many.

Only a person with faith can discern the difference. A poor man with faith will rejoice in the blessings of his riches in Christ, but a poor man who doubts will envy the rich and be bitter toward God for withholding wealth from him. A wealthy man with faith will be humbled by the added trials of his riches to use his wealth for the glory of God, but the rich man who doubts will ignore God and spend his wealth on his pleasures instead. Faith draws us to God to receive His blessings, but doubt pulls us away from God and deprives us of His blessings.

The truth is that God loves all of His children through faith in Jesus Christ and always blesses us out of the abundance of His grace far beyond what any of us really deserve. Even when we don't live by faith and do struggle with doubts, God continues to bless us in some measure, but He reserves His best blessings for those who keep faith through trials without doubting. The phrase "for once he has been approved" in verse 12 means once we have passed the test. Trials test us! They prove the sincerity and quality of our faith and how much we really love and trust God.

When we persevere through a trial with our faith and love for God intact and even strengthened, we get an A on the test and God's promise of the "crown of life." Some Bible scholars have suggested this speaks of a heavenly crown, of being crowned with rewards in heaven, but not all crowns mentioned in the Bible are heavenly crowns. For instance, Proverbs 12:4 says that an excellent wife is the crown of her husband. Amen, I completely agree. My wife is certainly my better half, and if I didn't admit it, she would probably want to "crown me" in a completely different sense, if you know what I mean. Proverbs 16:31 says that a gray head is a crown of glory. Now I don't feel so bad about getting older. Psalm 103:4 says that God crowns us with loving-kindness and compassion.

The point is that some crowns are for right here on earth, so a better understanding of the "crown of life" is that those who don't doubt God in trials will be crowned with a richer spiritual life here on earth. Think about it: if we trust God through trials and don't doubt Him, James has already taught us that we will not just endure them, but we will rejoice through them, recognize the good in them, draw closer to God to grow wiser because of them, and gain the added blessings of God's approval. That doesn't sound half-bad! It sounds like the kind of spiritual life all of us would love to be crowned with.

Doubters, however, will be a basket case in trials, paralyzed with indecision, unanswered prayers, without a clear purpose in life, blind to how God does bless them, and deprived of the special blessing of God's approval.

What kind of spiritual life is that? Which spiritual life would you like to be crowned with? It's up to us. It's ours to choose whether we handle trials by faith or we give in to doubt.

> And without faith it is impossible to please Him,
> for he who comes to God must believe that He is
> and that He is a rewarder of those who seek Him.
> (Hebrews 11:6)

WRONG WAY, DO NOT ENTER!

(James 1:13–14)

I'm a "country boy" and thus very uncomfortable driving on downtown city streets, especially when many of them only run one way. I must admit that I once unknowingly turned down a one-way street and had to make a quick correction. Luckily, it was not a busy street and there was no oncoming traffic, so a quick U-turn solved the problem. However, going the wrong way can sometimes have tragic consequences. Not long ago, I read about a driver speeding up an exit ramp of a major interstate straight into oncoming traffic, resulting in both his own death and that of a whole family in the vehicle he hit head-on.

Perhaps going the wrong way has never happened to you, but it's likely that most of us have accidently, or even intentionally, ignored one-way arrows to go in the out lane or out the in lane while coming or going from a fast-food joint. Even more likely, if not with certainty, all of us have ignored the "Wrong Way, Do Not Enter!" warnings of the Holy Spirit to drive head-on into temptations.

Temptations are something that we all face but that far too few really understand. It stands to reason that if we don't understand temptations, not only will we be more prone to succumb to them, but we'll also tend to think that it isn't really our fault when we do.

As a pastor and a Navy chaplain, I regularly have people come to me who are suffering the consequences of giving in to one temptation or another, and more often than not, they try to point a finger of blame in one of three directions. Either they point the finger at some sort of peer pressure that led them into sin, claim that "the devil made me do it" as if they had no choice in the matter, or are mad at God for letting them get into trouble because He could have prevented the circumstances they believe caused them to fail.

James 1:13–14 says that none of those options are correct and asserts in no uncertain terms that we will never conquer temptations until we first learn to point the finger of blame right back at ourselves. The real power of any temptation we face doesn't come from any force or person outside of us but entirely from the desires we already harbor within. In order to be tempted by something, it has to seem appealing to us; it has to "turn on" a desire we already have inside of us. So when we fail to resist a temptation and fall into sin, we can't blame anyone or anything else because it was our own sinful desire that made it seem so attractive.

Two words are used in this passage to describe the dynamic of every temptation. The first word is translated as "carried away" or "dragged away," and the second word is translated as "enticed," which comes from the root word for *bait*.

Being from Galilee, James was very familiar with fishing and uses it to describe how temptations work on us. Like a hungry fish lured to tasty bait, caught on a hook, and reeled in, so our inner desire or hunger for sin's bait (sinful, yes, but it looks good, smells good, feels good, or seems like it would be fun or exciting) attracts us to bite on sin's hidden hook, and we're caught and reeled in.

Now the devil, or peer pressure, might supply the bait and dangle it before our eyes, but they can't make us bite; so whose fault is it when we do? We are solely responsible for our failure because we wouldn't bite unless we already had a hunger for that sin.

Sure, the devil is a master at knowing just what bait to use and how to disguise the hook within. He can make sin seem so good and so harmless, until you take the bait, he has his hook in you, and you find out too late that it's a painful trap. But we can't blame God for being hooked. He's a fisherman too, but He never baits us with sin. His only bait is love and the good news of His salvation; so when you fail, don't blame God, or the devil, or point a finger at anyone else. You only have yourself to blame because you made the choice to swallow it "hook, line, and sinker."

> No temptation has overtaken you but such as is common to man; and God is faithful, who will not allow you to be tempted beyond what you are able, but with the temptation will provide the way of escape also, so that you will be able to endure it (1 Corinthians 10:13).

REV YOUR ENGINES

(JAMES 1:15–16)

Y ou're stopped at a red light when some guy pulls up alongside you in a flashy car, revs his engine to get your attention, and challenges you to a race. In your head, you know it's wrong, and it's reckless and dangerous; but in the heat of the moment, something in your competitive nature resonates like a tuning fork. You have a fast car too, and pride beckons a more aggressive response than just passive surrender. So when the light changes to green, you squeal the tires and you're off to the races. Well, maybe it wasn't quite that dramatic, but you were both in a hurry and two lanes were merging into one on the other side of the intersection; and both of you were determined to be the guy in front, so the race was on anyway. Congratulations! You just gave in to a temptation and gave birth to a healthy, bouncing baby sin.

That's the lesson of James 1:15–16. Being tempted is not a sin. Jesus was tempted by the devil, but He never sinned because he never entertained or acted on it. It's only when a temptation is yielded to or acted upon that a sin is committed. If someone dangles some bait to sin before your eyes but you reject it and turn away from it, you have not sinned. By faith, in righteousness, you recognized evil and walked away. This is how we should always flee from temptations.

James makes this clear with another great illustration from nature. He says temptations that lead to sin are a lot like conception. Just as there must be an act of sex to conceive a child, who then develops in the womb and is born, so a temptation, united with an act to fulfill it, gives birth to sin. Temptations give birth to sin whenever we reach out in some way to gratify or fulfill the lust we have inside us that the temptation appeals to, and reaching out is not limited to just physically reaching in some way. Sin is also born when we reach out with our minds to seriously entertain and fantasize about it. It might be sin in its infancy, but it's still a sin born kicking and screaming for our attention.

This is how most adultery takes place. No physical affair takes place, but lust is still gratified by fantasizing about it. The sin is conceived and gives birth as soon as our lust begins to be gratified in our minds, and the problem with newborn sin is that it naturally wants to grow up into something bigger and bigger as time goes on.

Baby sins grow up to be serial killers! Apart from receiving the grace of God through faith in Jesus Christ for forgiveness and eternal life, sin will lead to eternal death in hell for every unbeliever (Romans 6:23). Even for those of us who have received Jesus Christ and know our sin is forgiven, sin still has fatal consequences. Sin kills our self-worth and fills us with grief and shame. Sin kills our reputation and our effectiveness to testify our faith in Jesus Christ. Sin kills relationships, marriages, and the feeling of love and security our children would gain from growing up in a whole and loving family. Sin kills!

By confessing our sins and asking for God's forgiveness He can and does in His grace resurrect and bring new life to what our sin has killed, but the consequences of our sin can often remain for the rest of our lives. "Do not be deceived, my beloved brethren." Don't take the bait! Don't even think about moving in to take a closer look or reaching out to just touch it thinking, *I won't be hooked*. Famous last words! The hook will be set, sin will be born, and it will surely kill something in your life.

There's a *Frank and Ernest* comic strip about temptations that's quite insightful. Frank and Ernest are leaving church, and as they stop to shake the pastor's hand, Frank says, "We don't need to be led into temptations. We already know all the shortcuts." Indeed, we do! The shortcuts already lie within us, but as believers in Jesus Christ, so does the Holy Spirit. The voice of our own lusts says, "Do it! Go for it!" But the voice of the Holy Spirit is also always present, warning us not to take the bait. Luke 4:1 says that Jesus was "full of the Holy Spirit" and was "led around by the Spirit in the wilderness for forty days, being tempted by the devil." It was in the power of the Holy Spirit that Jesus was able to resist every temptation the devil threw at Him. That same power of the Spirit dwells in every believer and gives us the ability to do the same.

We will always have the witness of the Holy Spirit saying a firm "No!" to every temptation we face, which means we will always have the choice and power to also say, "No!" and turn away. Living by faith is all about choices, isn't it? And the choices we face every day, especially to say, "No!" to temptations, are always opportunities to say, "Yes!" to God.

> Therefore, since we have a great high priest who has passed through the heavens, Jesus the Son of God, let us hold fast our confession. For we do not have a high priest who cannot sympathize with our weaknesses, but One who has been tempted in all things as *we are, yet* without sin. Therefore, let us draw near with confidence to the throne of grace, so that we may receive mercy and find grace to help in time of need. (Hebrews 4:14–16)

YOUR FIRST CAR

(James 1:17a)

I don't know about you, but I couldn't wait till my sixteenth birthday so I could run down to the DMV and get my learner's permit to drive. I didn't grow up in a wealthy home, so I was not among those few kids who get to wake up to the gift of a brand-new car in the driveway tied with a great big bow. However, my father did help me purchase a very used 1966 VW Bug for $300. It was a real rust bucket, but it ran great and I spent many hours repairing the rust spots to make it something I was proud to drive and call my own. Many years later, when I was the dad, it was my joy to also help my two children buy their first cars. Like my own, they were used cars that had some rust and needed some work, but I think both my kids would tell you they look back on those first cars with fondness as I think most of us do.

As loving parents, whether a big gift like a car or a smaller gift, we enjoy giving good gifts to our children, seeing their excitement, and watching their joy as they unwrap and delight over them. This is even truer of our heavenly Father. Jesus said,

> Or what man is there among you, who when his son asks for a loaf, will give him a stone? Or if he asks for a fish, he will not give him a snake will he? If you then, being evil [a sinner], know how to give good gifts to your children, how much more will your Father who is in heaven give what is good to those who ask Him! (Matthew 7:9–11).

This truth is echoed in James 1:17, which says, "Every good thing given and every perfect gift is from above." In other words, God is the ultimate giver of ultimate gifts. First of all, because God's gifts are always good! He is the source and giver of everything that is good. Whatever good exists in the world and whatever good we have in our lives is only there because God gave it to us. Apart from God, good could not even exist!

This is a truth about God that so many people choose to ignore. Whenever something bad happens to them, they are quick to blame God; but when their lives are full of goodness, they fail to praise God. You can't have it both ways. If you blame God when bad things happen, then shouldn't you at least thank God for all the good things in your life?

Besides, who says that the "bad" things that happen to us are really bad? If God is good and He only gives good gifts to His children, doesn't that mean that the trials and temptations He allows us to face must be good? The Apostle Paul thought the trial of his "thorn in the flesh" was bad, and he prayed fervently for God to remove it; but God said no, and Paul was humbled to learn that God's grace was sufficient and what he couldn't do in the weakness of his flesh God could. The thorn was good!

Jesus was tempted by the devil, and while we all agree the devil is bad, was it bad that Jesus was tempted? No, it was good that He was "tempted in all things as we are, yet without sin," because it proved Him to be the sinless Son of God and the only worthy sacrifice for our sins. The temptation was good! Likewise, when we resist temptation, we too win a victory over the devil, and victory is good.

Second, God's gifts are always perfect! The word *perfect* is the same word used back in verse 4 for how God uses trials to grow our faith into all it needs to be to make us mature, well-rounded, and complete Christians. It means the same thing here in regard to God's gifts. God's gifts are always perfectly suited to the recipient. They are always given at the right time and in the right measure to completely meet the need of the one who receives it.

Let me give you a great example. After graduating from Grace Theological Seminary in 1988, I was called to pastor a small church in Friend, Nebraska. We had a severe hailstorm with some quarter-sized hail, which pretty much destroyed the roof of the church. We couldn't afford the thousands it would take to hire a contractor to replace the roof, but we had some men in the church who knew how to lay shingles. We got a quote from the building supply store that it would cost $2000 for the materials. The problem was that we didn't have $2000 either, so we prayed.

Someone suggested that we contact our insurance company to see if they would cover the damage. Well, the roof was more than thirty years old and already in bad shape before the storm, so none of us thought there was any chance we'd get anything out of an insurance claim; but the adjuster came, looked over the roof, and said he'd let us know. We prayed some more!

Our need was $2000. Did God provide $1000? No! $1500, No! $1999.99, No! Several days later, we received an insurance check for $2000.01. I'm convinced that God added the penny just to make a point, just to dispel any thought that it was all just a coincidence.

But that's not all. Unknown to me, my home church in western New York, where I received God's call into ministry, was looking for a summer, short-term mission project and, hearing of our need, sent a team out to help us put the new roof on. What would have taken a few men in the church weeks to accomplish was done in just a few days.

God's gifts are always good, but they're also always exactly what we need, when we need it, and perfectly suited to us and our situation. God's gifts always fully meet the need of the moment and never leave us lacking.

> And my God will supply all your needs according to His riches in glory in Christ Jesus. (Philippians 4:19)

HIGH BEAM HEADLIGHTS

(JAMES 1:17B–18)

The year 1966 was the last year that VW Bugs had a 6-volt electrical system. The one disadvantage of a 6-volt system, I quickly learned, was that the headlights were not nearly as bright as those on 12-volt American cars. Even while using my high beams, I found driving at night to be a much greater challenge because my headlights just didn't pierce the darkness and chase away the moving shadows along the sides of the road like the lights on my Dad's Buick. I had to drive slower, which, now that I think of it, may have been part of the "method to the madness" of my dad encouraging me to buy the VW instead of a V8-powered muscle car.

In His giving of good and perfect gifts, James refers to God as the "Father of lights, with whom there is no variation or shifting shadow." Have you ever read that and wondered what it has to do with God's gift giving?

Father of lights is a reference to God as the Creator of the heavenly bodies that give light to the earth. Genesis 1:14–16 says, "Then God said, Let there be lights in the expanse of the heavens to separate the day from the night…to give light on the earth; and it was so. And God made the two great lights, the greater light to govern the day, and the lesser light to govern the night; He made the stars also." Psalm 136 adds that the year-after-year constancy and reliability of these lights is rooted in the everlasting nature of our Creator.

> To Him who made the great lights,
> for His lovingkindness is everlasting:
> The sun to rule by day,
> For His lovingkindness is everlasting,
> The moon and stars to rule by night,
> For His lovingkindness is everlasting.
> (Psalm 136:7–9)

This reminds us that God's gifts aren't just good and perfect. As the Father of the lights in the sky is everlasting, so His gifts are also everlasting; and as the lights of the heavens are fixed upon the skies, so His gifts are permanently fixed upon us.

However, James is quick to point out that even the consistency of the sun and moon is a less-than-perfect illustration of the lasting and unchanging character of God and His gifts because their light casts shadows that are constantly changing. Shadows vary in shape and size as the sun moves across the sky from east to west. Shadows stretch far to the west as the sun rises in the east and shrink to almost nothing at noon and then grow longer toward the east as the sun sets in the west.

God is not like that! His nature, His character, and thus His gifts are unchanging. He doesn't give a gift at one moment only to capriciously take it back in the next. Hebrews 13:8 says, "Jesus is the same yesterday and today and forever." Therefore, so are the gifts He pours out on those of us who have placed our faith in Jesus Christ. "For the gifts and the calling of God are irrevocable" (Romans 11:29).

Finally, God's gifts are proven! It says in verse 18 that God's good, perfect, and everlasting gifts are proven most conclusively by His desire to save sinners. As James writes from his early church perspective, God's choice to save him and the first-century Christians he was directly writing to is likened to the first fruits of a greater harvest of all who would be born again in subsequent centuries. These early believers were just the earliest fruit of what would be a bumper crop of saved souls by the time God was done saving all He has chosen to save.

And now almost 2000 years removed from James, this is exactly what we see. From the time of James on, Christianity transformed the world. It turned the Roman Empire from polytheism to Christ. In just a few centuries, Christianity became the foundation upon which all of the free world was built. The book of Revelation even gives us a peek into the future when it speaks of the great multitude of believers who will be in heaven and describes them as "myriads of myriads, and thousands of thousands."

God is the ultimate giver because His gifts are always good, perfect, and everlasting as proven by His greatest gift of all—the gift of salvation. A gift still free for the taking to anyone who will confess that they're a sinner, believe that Jesus Christ was God in the flesh who came to earth to be the sinless and only sacrifice for sin and rose from the dead to prove it, and ask Him to forgive their sin and give them everlasting life.

Why would anyone choose to turn down the ultimate giver's ultimate gift?

> If you confess with your mouth Jesus *as* Lord, and believe in your heart that God raised Him from the dead, you will be saved; for with the heart a person believes, resulting in righteousness, and with the mouth he confesses, resulting in salvation. (Romans 10:9–10)

ATTITUDES BEHIND THE WHEEL (PART 1)

(JAMES 1:19–20)

R ead any state's DMV driver's manual or take just about any "safe driver" class, and you will be warned about maintaining right attitudes while driving. Though some specifics may vary, they generally boil down to respect and responsibility. Let's consider respect first. Every driver should have respect for the law in order to obey the "rules of the road," and we should also have respect for others and extend courtesy to those who share the road with us.

Tracie and I share a little joke between us whenever we get stuck behind some slowpoke or are slowed down by heavy traffic. One or the other of us will say, "Didn't they get the memo that we would be on the road and they are supposed to stay home till we go by?" We're not serious, of course, but just trying to lighten the mood. The truth is that others have just as much right to the road as we do, and just as we're taught to share our toys as children, we must also generously share the road with fellow drivers.

Second, we must take full responsibility for our driving. For instance, if I'm getting frustrated and hot under the collar because I'm running late and get stuck behind a slowpoke or held up in traffic, it's not the fault of the other drivers around me. It's my fault for not anticipating traffic and getting an early-enough start. I'm responsible!

Having respect and accepting responsibility makes us better drivers. Just think how much smoother and less stressful driving would be if we all maintained these attitudes behind the wheel.

Well, in the same way that respect is essential to safety on the road, it is also essential to how we read God's Word, receive His truth, and live out His gift of salvation. First, we must always approach God's Word with the greatest of respect manifested by our willingness to be "quick to hear, slow to speak, and slow to anger."

God's Word deserves an anxious readiness on our part to listen. Rather than view God's Word with reluctance, avoidance, or neglect, we should be eager and excited to give it our prompt and regular attention. Our Bibles should never just collect dust on some shelf.

On my first deployment to Iraq, during the eight months I was away from home, Tracie wrote me seventy-two letters. We had no e-mail at all for the first three months and very little access to what few computers we had for the last five months. It was snail mail or practically nothing, and those love letters from Tracie were my lifeline. I couldn't wait to get mail and read those letters over and over. I did pretty well myself and wrote her over fifty letters, and she was just as anxious to read my love letters back to her.

That's how anxious we should be to read the Bible. It's a collection of God's love letters to us that we should want to read over and over again. It is our lifeline to our heavenly Father. Most people are quick to avoid the Bible, but as God's children, we should be quick to read it and hear what God has say to us.

Respect also demands that we be slow to speak. Reading God's word requires restrained speech. The idea here is not to be argumentative with the Word of God. Our reception of the Word should be quiet obedience rather than trying to talk our way out of or around it. This is what we're tempted to do, isn't it? We hear God's truth convicting us of some sin in our lives, and we make excuses and try to argue our way around it. "I didn't do it. It wasn't my fault. So-and-so made me do it. It was only a little white lie. It's not that big a deal."

I remember doing a lot of arguing with God when I began to sense He was calling me into the ministry. I'd read the Scriptures or hear a message on Sunday morning calling me out to serve and spend the next few days thinking of every reason I could why I shouldn't go. "I have a family to take care of. I can't quit a good job and go back to school. Where would I get the money? What if, after I finish school, God calls me to some part of the world I don't really want to go to?" Yeah, like Iraq or Afghanistan.

Ever done that, argue with the conviction of God's Word? When we do that, we're not really receiving the Word, are we? James says that rather than be quick to talk yourself out of what the Bible says, we should slow down, be quiet, and let God continue to do the talking.

Anger is the natural progression from the argumentative attitude James just warned about in being slow to speak. What happens when we can't talk ourselves out of whatever conviction we're feeling and the conviction persists? Do we submit to the Word of God and obey, or do we get mad, or maybe even both? We obey, but we're mad about it.

Who likes to be told they're wrong? Who enjoys being accused of sin, even if told in love? No, we resist! First, we don't want to listen. Second, we usually try to deny it. If that doesn't work, we argue to justify ourselves; and if, that doesn't work, we get mad at the messenger and maybe even mad at God. And what does that get us? Ask Jonah! It got him an up-close and personal encounter with a great fish that reduced him from prophet of God to fish vomit, and even after that, he still stayed angry.

Thank God He rarely goes to such extremes to deal with our anger. But ask yourself, "What good has my anger at the truth or at God ever accomplished?" I bet the answer is a big, fat goose egg, which is why James says, "For the anger of man does not achieve the righteousness of God." An angry attitude toward the Word of God will not allow righteousness to flourish in our lives. Anger actually closes our minds to the truth.

Think about it. When have you ever been angry and open-minded at the same time? Anger is very narrow-minded. When have you ever been angry and teachable at the same time? Anger closes our spirit and keeps us from learning. I like the way the NIV translates this verse. It says, "For man's anger does not bring about the righteous life that God desires." Anger keeps us from receiving the truth and growing in righteousness, so we must be very careful not to get angry when the truth hurts.

> He who is slow to anger is better than the mighty,
> and he who rules his spirit, than he who captures
> a city. (Proverbs 16:32)

ATTITUDES BEHIND THE WHEEL (PART 2)

(JAMES 1:21)

In the previous chapter, we discussed the importance of respect. This evidence of respect for God's Word must then be followed up with responsibility. As safe drivers, we must always take full responsibility for our driving. As I stated in the previous chapter, if I'm getting frustrated and hot under the collar because I'm running late and get stuck behind a slowpoke or held up in traffic, it's not the fault of the other drivers around me. It's my fault for not anticipating traffic and getting an early-enough start. I'm responsible! Just think how much smoother and less stressful driving would be if we all accepted full responsibility for our actions and attitudes behind the wheel.

Likewise, if you want to read the Bible for all its worth, you have to be fully responsible for how you respond to God's truth. The phrase *putting aside* comes from the word used for undressing, taking off your clothes. The idea is that in order to fully receive God's Word, we must take off and lay aside whatever hangs on us as excess weight that might keep us from fully acting on the truth. It's the same word used in Hebrews 12:1, which says, "Therefore, since we have so great a cloud of witnesses surrounding us, let us also *lay aside* every encumbrance and the sin which so easily entangles us, and let us run with endurance the race that is set before us." The idea is to strip off any excess weight or baggage, such as unnecessary clothes, in order to run a race unhindered.

Picture it like this: We don't go to the gym to work out in layers and layers of clothes. They would weigh us down and hinder our movement. We strip down to just shorts and a T-shirt so we can move faster and easier. Sin is our excess weight or baggage that hinders us from fully receiving the truth and running for God. We have to turn away from it and strip it away for our faith to be unhindered.

The word *filthiness* refers to idolatrous practices, or anything in our lives we might place above God, and *wickedness* refers to that which is immoral. Sin weighs us down. It hinders us from moving forward with God until we repent of the wrong and remove that sin from our thinking and behavior, and that takes humility. "In humility, receive the word implanted, which is able to save your souls." Just as the Word of God convicted us as sinners and humbled us to trust Christ and accept Him as Lord and Savior to receive salvation, we need to let God's Word continue to humble us as believers to progressively strip away more and more of the sin that still clings to us and hinders our faith. Only a humble spirit can fully receive God's Word and let it do its work of change in our lives. We can't fully receive the truth unless we take responsibility to admit our faults, confess our sins, and submit our will to God's will instead.

God has given us His Word to do so much more than just save us. Salvation is just the beginning of His work in our lives. God says His Word is like fire that burns away the dross to refine us. It's like a hammer that beats us on God's anvil to shape us into something fit for glory. His Word is training in righteousness to perfect and complete our faith to be remade in the likeness of Jesus Christ. But it can't happen unless we read it for all its worth. Our challenge is to be in the Word often and immerse ourselves in its pages, not just with a shallow reading, but always with respect that is quick to hear, slow to speak, and slow to anger, followed by our responsibility to humbly repent and let God refine us, shape us, and remake us into the holy, fully mature men or women of God He has created us to be.

> For this reason we also constantly thank God that when you received the word of God which you heard from us, you accepted *it* not *as* the word of men, but *for* what it really is, the word of God, which also performs its work in you who believe. (1 Thessalonians 2:13)

PRACTICE MAKES PERFECT

(James 1:22–25)

Like most teenage boys, I wasted no time on my sixteenth birthday getting down to the DMV to take the written test and get my learner's permit to drive, and with the permit tucked neatly in my wallet, my mother even let me drive home. Being taught that "practice makes perfect," I took advantage of every opportunity possible to get behind the wheel so I would be ready to take the driving test to get my license.

Driving came quite easy to me, but the only thing I had any concern about on the driving test was the requirement to parallel park. It's not something most of us do very often, so it's the one thing I practiced the most. The old adage once again turned out to be true because during the test, I performed it flawlessly and proudly received my license.

Practice does make perfect! Most of us heard that old saying growing up, and most of us have probably quoted that to our children as well. As a general rule, this has been accepted as truth for thousands of years. Well, what works to develop the skills to drive and parallel park is also just as necessary for every Christian to hone the skills and reflexes necessary to live out our faith.

James is inspired by the Holy Spirit to tell us why practice is so important to living by faith. First of all, he says in verse 22, practice proves our faith. Talk is cheap, and actions speak louder than words. It's easy to say we believe in something, but the real proof is in whether we live by what we say we believe.

I can go around all day professing that I can break the world record in the long jump, but just saying it doesn't prove I really can; and you'd be crazy to believe me unless you actually saw me do it. Likewise, many people profess faith in Christ but show no real lifestyle change to back up what they say they believe.

Now, even as believers, we still sin, and all of us struggle with some issues in our lives that contradict our faith. None of us can live out our faith perfectly 100% of the time, but James isn't suggesting that. However, he is saying that our profession of faith in Jesus Christ should be evidenced every day by how we live.

Jesus says in Luke 6:46–49,

> Why do you call Me, "Lord, Lord," and do not do what I say? Everyone who comes to Me and hears My words and acts on them, I will show you whom he is like: he is like a man building a house, who dug deep and laid a foundation on the rock; and when a flood occurred, the torrent burst against that house and could not shake it, because it had been well built. But the one who has heard and has not acted *accordingly*, is like a man who built a house on the ground without any foundation; and the torrent burst against it and immediately it collapsed, and the ruin of that house was great.

Putting God's Word into practice in our lives, not just saying we believe God's Word is true but living by its truths, is the proof that we really believe. Yes, we are saved by faith alone apart from good works, absolutely! But doing the Word is what proves the quality and seriousness of our faith. Practice proves our faith!

Second, practice builds spiritual muscle memory (verse 22). Having been a Marine Corps infantry battalion chaplain, I can tell you with absolute confidence that Marines practice a lot. They train all the time. Why? So that when they hear a command, the appropriate action is almost automatic. They barely have to think about it because all the practice has so trained their minds and bodies that running toward danger and engaging the enemy has become second nature. It's just their reflex to accomplish the mission no matter what it takes.

As Christians, should we do any less? How can we ever hope to fight the spiritual battles of our faith if we don't practice? Practice tunes our ears to hear the command of God to be His witnesses and respond with a good testimony. It sharpens our senses to look out for the devil's ambushes of temptation so we can immediately lay down a crossing field of fire of God's truth to kill our own lust to surrender to sin. It prepares us to come to the aid of a fellow believer wounded by sin so we can lovingly bind up their wounds and carry them off the battlefield, rather than leave them behind with judgment and indignation.

If we say we believe in Jesus as our Lord but we don't strive to practice His Word to prove our faith and build spiritual muscle memory, then Jesus and James both say we're just fooling ourselves; we've deluded ourselves into some form of "easy believism" that can say one thing and do another.

Third, practice reveals and corrects our flaws (verses 23–24). James is a master of illustration, and here, he likens the Word of God to a mirror. Just like a mirror reflects a true image of our physical appearance (our "natural face," he says), so the Word of God will reflect the kind of person we really are on the inside. When we look at ourselves in the mirror of God's truth, it reveals the good, the bad, and the ugly of our true self in uncomfortable detail.

Hebrews 4:12 says, "For the Word of God is living and active and sharper than any two-edged sword, and piercing as far as the division of soul and spirit, of both joints and marrow, and able to judge the thoughts and intentions of the heart." The Word of God reveals and reflects back to us the image of our very souls, pleasant or unpleasant, attractive or unattractive as it may be.

James explains that the person who only hears the Word of God, in one ear and out the other, is just like a person who looks in a mirror and sees that her hair is a mess, her makeup is smudged, or he has food stuck in his teeth, and a booger hanging out of his nose (is that graphic enough?); and he or she walks away from the mirror without trying to fix what was wrong.

No one in their right mind would do that, but that's exactly what we all do when we ignore the faults the Word of God reveals about us and we do nothing to correct them. God's Word reflects the image of our unkempt souls so we will do something about it and ask God to carry out the repairs and renovations needed. The Word will always reflect a true image of our soul, but it's only by putting the Word into practice that God will give us the extreme makeover we all need. Only practice can prove our faith, build spiritual muscle memory, and reveal and correct our flaws.

Finally, practice frees us to experience God's blessing (verse 25). God's Word deserves much more than just a shallow glance or cursory look. It's not for skim reading to be taken lightly as many people seem to do. It requires careful study and deep thought. *Looks intently* refers to concentrated attention and describes a doer of the Word as having such an intense interest in what God has to say that he or she will scrutinize and be deeply absorbed in its truth.

When people give the Bible a shallow look or just half-hearted attention, they end up with a faulty notion that just breaks it down into a list of dos and don'ts that will be incorrectly applied in one of two ways. Either they will reject all the rules because they feel like God doesn't want them to have any fun, or they'll become legalistic adherents to the rules who mistakenly believe they can earn salvation by religiously keeping them; both these ways lead straight to hell.

However, those who "look intently," who dig deep, understand that God's Word is not a list of rules to keep. It is a "declaration of independence" that frees us from the law of rules that only condemn us as rule breakers so we can abide in the liberty of God's blessings of forgiveness and grace in Jesus Christ. Think of it like this: when I was deployed to Iraq and Afghanistan, I lived on a fixed operating base (FOB) surrounded by walls, concertina wire, and guard towers. Did we resent the barriers? Did we think they were there to hem us in, cramp our style, and make sure we couldn't have any fun? No! The barriers were there to keep the enemy out and us safe. They allowed us to sleep in peace and gave us freedom of movement to live and work inside the wire of protection.

That's the blessing of God's Word for those who practice at studying and abiding in its truths. Does it put up some barriers? Yes, but only to keep our mortal enemy of sin away from us and keep it from hurting us. Other than that, it's all liberty to enjoy the blessings of a relationship with God as our loving heavenly Father, our Savior, our protector, and our friend.

"Practice makes perfect!" It's really only true if what we practice is the "perfect law, the law of liberty" we call the Bible—God's Holy Word. Many people hear the Word, but far fewer do anything with it. Are you merely a hearer, or are you a doer? Do you just hear the truth, or are you a practitioner of the truth?

Without practice, our faith is unproven. Without practice, we will never build any spiritual muscle memory that makes righteousness second nature. Without practice, our faults and flaws will never be corrected. Without practice, we will miss out on so much of the blessing God wants to pour out on us.

> Finally, brethren, whatever is true, whatever is honorable, whatever is right, whatever is pure, whatever is lovely, whatever is of good repute, if there is any excellence and if anything worthy of praise, dwell on these things...practice these things, and the God of peace will be with you. (Philippians 4:8–9)

THE TROUBLE WITH TECHNOLOGY

(JAMES 1:26–27)

Cars are so much more complicated than they used to be. I remember when an owner's manual used to be a small booklet of just a few dozen pages. Now cars come with a warranty book, an owner's manual, and a supplemental instruction book detailing the use of the sound system, Bluetooth technology, and navigation apps all totaling more than 1000 pages! The truth is, I don't even know half the things my car is able to do and wouldn't want to take the time to read all the manuals to find out. Add to this all the new distractions that cell phones, texting, and video screens have added to driving and the accidents they've caused, I have to wonder if all this technology is really worth it.

In some ways, I think religion is a lot like technology. Technology is a wonderful thing when used to protect and improve our lives, but it can also make life unnecessarily complicated or even be used for evil to kill and enslave people; and so it can also be with religion. When religion is a demonstration of our faith in God according to His truth and expressed in acts of love, it is good; but religion has also been used to impose oppressive legalism, kill those who don't conform, and even attempt genocide against a whole people. This misuse of religion is really nothing new. James had to deal with this issue from the earliest days of Christianity, and he offers some practical truth to help us distinguish whether the religion we practice is pure or worthless.

If each of us were to go out this week and ask people the question "What do you think it means to be religious?" Many will say things like, I believe in God, I pray, I go to church, I was baptized (they practice rituals or liturgies of the church), and I try to be a good person. Most people equate being religious with a church and the acts of devotion associated with that particular faith tradition, and all of these acts are good, if done according to God's Word and motivated by a faith relationship with Jesus Christ as Lord and Savior. But unfortunately, it's also easy for people to fall into the trap of performing religious acts out of tradition and habit, more out of devotion to the church itself than as a true expression of faith in Christ.

God admonishes Israel for this very "going through the motions" kind of religion in Isaiah 29:13, which says,

> Because this people draw near with their words and honor Me with their lip service, but they remove their hearts far from Me, and their reverence for Me consists of tradition learned *by rote*, Therefore behold, I will once again deal marvelously with this people, wondrously marvelous; and the wisdom of their wise men will perish, and the discernment of their discerning men will be concealed.

They performed all the right rituals and recited all the right words, but their hearts weren't really in it. Their faith, passion, and love for God had been replaced with habit, tradition, and going through the motions. God says it's worthless. It doesn't mean anything to Him, and because they'd chosen a dumbed-down faith, He would take away what little wisdom they had left.

This is where many people are today. They have religion, but they don't have a personal relationship with Jesus Christ. They're connected to their church but not really connected to God. They have a reverence for ritual and tradition but not the Lordship of Jesus Christ that asks them to take up the cross daily and follow Him. Pure religion has to be more than just performing acts of religious tradition.

Pure religion should be life changing! A pure religion based on faith in Jesus Christ as Lord and Savior can't help but radically transform us in three key areas: The first being our character as demonstrated by how we use our tongue. Nothing will betray our true character and is harder to control than our tongue. Wouldn't you agree? It is with the tongue that we lie and practice deceit. It is with the tongue that we selfishly blame others for our own faults. It is the tongue that expresses our unrighteous anger, gossip, insults, adulterous flirtations, and self-righteous judgments of others. Our tongue is what most quickly and clearly reveals the character of our heart.

Jesus makes this abundantly clear in Matthew 15:1–20. After quoting Isaiah 29:13 to condemn the traditions-based, going-through-the-motions religion of the scribes and Pharisees, Jesus says,

> Listen and understand. What goes into someone's mouth does not defile them, but what comes out of their mouth, that is what defiles them...the things that proceed out of the mouth come from the heart, and those defile the man. For out of the heart come evil thoughts, murders, adulteries, fornications, thefts, false witness, slanders. These are the things which defile the man.

Pure religion affects a change of heart. It confronts these sins of character and demands change. It doesn't allow us to remain comfortable practicing these sins, but convicts us to repent and gives us the desire and power of God's Word and the Holy Spirit to begin the lifelong process of change. It doesn't happen all at once. It takes time, but we grow in character until our hearts beat more and more in tune with God's heart. If a person's religion doesn't effect a positive and lasting change of heart, then God says this person's religion is worthless.

Pure religion not only transforms our character but also changes our priorities. Pure religion helps us transition from looking out only for ourselves to also looking out for others. God was so wise to sum up the whole law as loving God and loving your neighbor as yourself, because the one thing we all tend to do very well is love ourselves, look out for number 1, and be concerned just with me and mine.

Being religious can even bolster our self-love and encourage us to feel pretty good about ourselves for being such a good person. I'm saved, I'm forgiven, God loves me—too bad for the other guy. And so many people make their way to church occasionally, or even every Sunday, with hardly a thought for the lost or less fortunate, and in some cases maybe even looking down on others for not being as "holy" as they are. God says, if that's how your religion makes you feel, it's worthless!

God illustrates this with orphans and widows because they were the most vulnerable and helpless of people in the society of James's day. If a woman was widowed and her husband did not leave her with the financial means to eat, keep a house, and pay the bills, she had about five options: (1) Hope her children or other family members would take her in, if she had any. (2) Marry anybody who would have her, not for love but just to survive. (3) Sell herself into slavery, if she was healthy enough to work. (4) Be forced into prostitution. (5) Become a beggar.

Orphans had it even worse. If family or some other caring person wouldn't take them in, they were on the street to fend for themselves. There were no orphanages, no state-run department of social services; they were on their own to become homeless little street urchins stealing whatever they could to survive.

God says, "Listen. If your religion can't even tug on your heart-strings to help a homeless kid, or a helpless widow, who will you help? What good is your religion if all you care about is you and yours?" Pure religion brings us down a notch or two and elevates others to a higher priority. Philippians 2:3–4 expresses this beautifully. It says,

"Do nothing from selfishness or empty conceit, but with humility of mind regard one another as more important than yourselves; do not *merely* look out for your own personal interests, but also for the interests of others." How we prioritize the needs and interests of others will say a lot about the purity of our religion.

Finally, the transforming quality of pure religion will produce in us a change in our worldview. When we trust Christ for forgiveness, He cleanses us from all our sin and clothes us with His righteousness. But this world is filthy with sin, and it's easy to let its filth rub off on us and soil who we are as children of God.

Mothers, how does it feel to dress up your children in their Sunday best only to have them go out and play and get their good clothes all dirty before church? That's how God feels when after He dresses us in His righteousness, we play with the world and get all dirty with sin.

How is it that so many people who claim to be Christians have so bought into the world's filthy values? Premarital sex, adultery, pornography, drunkenness, and filthy language are just a few examples of how the church and Hollywood are almost indistinguishable. These sins are almost as prevalent in the church as they are in the unbelieving world. Something is very wrong! Pure religion transforms; it changes a believer's worldview from accepting the world's filthy values to hating and shunning them. Worthless religion buys into the world's filthy values, but pure religion leads us away from the filth so it won't rub off on us and stain the name of Christ.

We sit in the comfort of our sanctuaries in Bible-preaching, gospel-proclaiming churches and chapels and want to think that James is talking about worthless churches that don't preach the gospel filled with professing Christians who aren't really saved. No, he's not! Remember, he's writing to believers, "beloved brethren," genuine "saved by faith in Jesus Christ" believers, whose religion is so weak and worthless they can sit in church on Sunday and make mud pies with the world the rest of the week.

Pure religion isn't about devotion to traditional rites and rituals; it's not about going through the motions of worship. Mark Twain said, "Having spent considerable time with good [religious] people, I can understand why Jesus liked to be with tax collectors and sinners." Mark Twain was certainly no saint, but he was absolutely right. The last thing the church or the world needs is more "religious" people. Don't ever make it your goal to be more religious; make it your ambition to be transformed by God into a living example of Jesus Christ.

> Do not be conformed to this world, but be transformed by the renewing of your mind, so that you may prove what the will of God is, that which is good and acceptable and perfect. (Romans 12:2)

DISCRIMINATING CAR OWNERS

(JAMES 2:1–13)

I don't think it's quite as prevalent as it used to be, but when I was growing up, many people seemed to hold a passionate loyalty to one particular car brand. I remember hearing Chevy people joke, "What does Ford stand for? *Found on road dead*." Then Ford people would counter, "What do you call five Chevys and a Ford? A junkyard and a ride home." It was mostly in good fun, but there was also a real prejudice for one car make or another. For instance, one of my grandpas always bought Fords, but my other gramps wouldn't buy anything but a Buick.

There's no doubt that all car makers advertise that their cars are better than their competitors' cars, but the truth is that all car makers make mostly good, reliable cars and all have made some lemons. However, car prejudice isn't just about reliability; some people drive expensive cars that boast of their social status, while others might prefer a fast, high-horsepower car to fulfill their ego's "need for speed."

There are a host of reasons why, but the fact remains that car buyers tend to be very discriminating about their purchases.

Well, when it comes to cars, prejudice for or against a particular make or model is fine; but when it comes to living out our faith in Jesus Christ, God says we must love without prejudice. In chapter 1 of James, we learned that real faith can be seen in how we handle trials, resist temptations, and receive the Word of God and in whether our religion is pure or we just act religious. Now, as we begin chapter 2, James focuses our attention on what is the quintessential expression of real faith—how we love others. Real faith loves without prejudice!

In verse 1, the Greek verb translated as "do not hold" is in what's called the present imperative tense, which is significant for two reasons. First, as a present tense verb, it's not just saying "don't do this," as if we haven't yet but we might in the future; no, it means to stop doing what we're already doing. Second, as an imperative verb, it holds the force of a command. When put together, James is getting right in the face of his readers and in the strongest language possible commanding them to "stop it! Stop showing favoritism! Stop practicing discrimination! Stop being so prejudiced!"

Now, why is this so serious that it needs such a strong rebuke? Because of who we are! Let's remember whom James is writing to— believers, his beloved brethren, those who "hold their faith in our glorious Lord Jesus Christ." As Christians, we have a serious responsibility to love others without prejudice.

It is also critical that we love without prejudice because of Whom we belong to! The phrase "our glorious Lord Jesus Christ" doesn't translate very well from Greek to English. Literally, it should be translated as "our Lord Jesus Christ—the Glory." The emphasis here isn't on Jesus just being glorious, but to the Jewish Christians James was directly writing to, "the Glory" is a powerful statement that Jesus Christ is the very glory of Almighty God—the Shekinah glory of the Jehovah God of the Old Testament.

Let's think about Jesus Christ, "the Glory," for a moment. Did He ever show prejudice or practice favoritism? No! He never favored Himself over others. Philippians 2:6–7 says that though He existed as God, He emptied Himself to become a man to die for us. Romans 15:3 says, "For even Christ did not please [favor] Himself, but as it is written, 'The reproaches of those who reproached you fell on Me.'" Jesus put Himself last to put us first.

He never favored one group of people over another. John 3:16 says, "For God so loved the *world* that He gave His only begotten Son that *whosoever* believes in Him shall not perish but have everlasting life." God is no respecter of persons. He sees us all the same as lost sinners in need of forgiveness and salvation. As the children's Sunday school song says, "Red and yellow, black and white, they're all precious in His sight. Jesus loves the little children of the world." "Whoever will call upon the Name of the Lord will be saved" (Romans 10:13).

He never favors one of His believing children over another. Galatians 3:28 says, "There is neither Jew nor Greek, there is neither slave nor free man, there is neither male nor female; for you are all one in Christ Jesus." There is no partiality or favoritism in the family of God. So why such a strong prohibition against prejudice? To love with prejudice is totally inconsistent with the God whom we claim to love and serve. It should never even be associated with faith in such an exalted person as Jesus Christ, the Glory, so God says, "Stop it!

Now that we understand God's prohibition against discrimination, let's look at the problems with discrimination. What is so evil, so sinful, so unloving about discrimination? First of all, it makes us judges. James illustrates this by pointing to discrimination based on wealth he had already seen being practiced in the church. The rich people got the best seats, and the poor had to stand or sit on the floor. The early church didn't meet in church sanctuaries like we do. Services were held in people's homes, where space was limited. Most likely, they were wealthier families who had bigger homes, and the homeowners were favoring their wealthier friends with the best seats in the house.

Wealth is only one superficial distinction, but the principle here holds true for any other personal bias used to favor one person over another. The point is that as Christians, we must never "judge a book by its cover," so to speak, and view another person on the basis of any personal prejudice. We should never judge others by some superficial impression we have about their position, rank, wealth, looks, talents, skin tone, sex, ethnic origin, age, religion, or any other superficial difference we can see. Our faith in Jesus Christ should see and show love to everyone as persons for whom Christ impartially died and desires to save.

To use some kind of personal prejudice to pick and choose whom to accept and help and share the gospel with makes us a judge of whether they are worthy of love and salvation and acceptance into the family of God, which is something only God can judge. That's why personal prejudices are called "evil motives," because they cause us to make judgments about people only God is qualified to make.

The second problem with prejudice is that it endorses false values. Being poor only makes a difference in the eyes of the world because its value system is materialistic; the more you have, the more important the world thinks you are. But God's value system is completely different. God doesn't judge us by how rich in this world's goods we are, but by the quality of our faith; to be rich in faith is what counts with God. James points out the inconsistency of placing value on wealth when, by and large, it was the rich who were blasphemously oppressing and persecuting Christians in his day, which is still true today. So for us to favor others based on their material status is to show a false value system contrary to God's.

And wealth is only one example of the world's false values. When we discriminate based on physical appearance, we also show false values, because it says in 1 Samuel 16:7 that God "sees not as man sees, for man looks at the outward appearance, but the Lord looks at the heart." So when we discriminate based on physical appearance, we're using a manmade value system, not God's. Or how about when we discriminate between people based on ability, inability, or disability? The world exalts those who seem to be more gifted, more capable. They are elevated to celebrity status and get special attention and privilege.

But God doesn't judge us by our abilities but by our availability, our willingness to use what abilities we do have for the glory of God. "As each one has received a gift, employ it in serving one another as good stewards of the manifold grace of God" (1 Peter 4:10). Jesus said that even offering a cup of cold water in Jesus's name was worthy of God's award. Think about it: any kind of discrimination we could engage in involves one of these three false values: exalting the material over the spiritual, exalting appearance over the heart, or exalting ability over availability. God's values are just the opposite, and ours should be too!

The third problem with discrimination is that it violates the royal law of love. Love is the key issue. To practice discrimination betrays the absence of a loving spirit. It violates God's commandment to "love your neighbor as yourself." The Golden Rule requires us to treat others the way we want to be treated. If you don't want to be discriminated against, then don't discriminate against others, because if you do, you will be guilty of the most serious of crimes.

The word *crime* is not an exaggeration. Prejudice isn't just some social "faux pas" or minor sin that can be overlooked. In the eyes of God, it is just as evil a crime as adultery or murder. Why? Because the whole law is summed up in loving God and loving your neighbor as yourself, which is why it's called the "royal law," and when we discriminate against others, we fail to love both them and the God in whose image they are created.

So failing to love without prejudice carries serious consequences. God does not discriminate between one sin and another; sin is sin and guilt is guilt, and God will judge us by the same measure that we have judged others. The more we love, the less we will be judged. The more we withhold mercy by harboring prejudice toward others, the more mercilessly God will judge us. The bottom line is, show love; be merciful because "mercy triumphs over judgment."

Do you harbor any prejudices? Perhaps we all have some. As the Holy Spirit prompts conviction, we need to confess it to the Lord, ask His forgiveness, and seek His help to stop it and let God fill us with His love and mercy toward others as those Jesus, the Glory, died for without any prejudice.

For there is no partiality with God. (Romans 2:11)

FENDER BENDER
TEST OF LOVE

(JAMES 2:14–26)

My parents were generous and supportive in letting us kids use the family car, so one night, I asked to borrow the car to go to my friend's house to hang out. It was a dark, rainy night, and as I was passing by a farm, a barnyard goose ran out in the road in front of me; and as I swerved to miss it, the car started into a fishtail skid. I immediately steered into the skid but came out of it a fraction too late and kissed the side of a metal bridge built over a creek. It was just enough to dent the front passenger fender and break both a headlight and a sidelight. If I had been driving my nimble VW Bug, I doubt the skid would've even happened, but my dad's Buick Electra was not so forgiving; and neither did I think my dad would be so forgiving when he found out what happened.

My dad had a pretty explosive temper, and I was prepared for a severe tongue-lashing and probably being grounded for the foreseeable future; but to my utter surprise, he just asked me what happened, looked at the damage, and said, "It's just a car. I'm just glad that you weren't hurt." Now I always believed that my dad loved me, but I guess it was never more real to me than by how he proved it with his gentle understanding and concern only for my safety.

"Actions speak louder than words." It isn't words alone that prove the depth of our love or the genuineness of our faith, but whether our attitudes and actions live up to our words. This is the decisive point of James 2:14–26. Faith acts! It should be visible and obvious. People should be able to look at us and see in our attitudes and actions the faith we profess to have in Jesus Christ. So what is faith? If faith is more than just words, then what does it look like?

First of all, we need to understand that this is *not* an argument for whether we're saved by faith, or works, or faith plus works. The Scriptures are clear that we are saved by faith alone apart from works. If you have any doubt, I encourage you to read John 6:28–29, Luke 23:39–43, Romans 3:28, Romans 4:4–5, Ephesians 2:8–9, 2 Timothy 1:9, Titus 3:5–6, and 1 Peter 1:3–5. James is not disputing or contradicting this precious truth in any way. He is simply pointing to the problem of seeing faith as a mere claim like, "Yeah, I believe in Jesus."

James's reply is, "Well that's nice. I'm glad you say you believe in Jesus, but can you back up your words? Do you have anything to show for it? Because if your faith isn't powerful enough to *work* change in your life for the glory of God on earth, why should you expect it to save your soul and get you to heaven?"

Makes sense, doesn't it! "You say you have faith in Jesus. Show me. I want to see it. Prove it to me." He's simply and rightfully arguing that if your faith is really saving faith, it has to be more than a mere profession of words. There has to be some evidence that backs up our words. It can't be without visible proof that it's working righteous changes in our lives. Amen!

So saving faith is more than just words, but what else does saving faith look like? God says it's also more than just an emotional response. James illustrates with something he'd no doubt personally observed in the church. He speaks of the person who seems sincerely moved by the plight of a brother or sister believer who doesn't have adequate clothes or food but whose concerns stop at just sympathy rather than tangible help.

Merely telling someone to stay warm and be fed doesn't put a coat on them or fill their stomach. It does them no good. If concern for the needs of others doesn't go beyond just feelings of sympathy, being sorry for them, no matter how sincere our emotions may be, it does nothing to actually help meet the need.

The same is true of faith. For many people, their faith is emotion without substance. It's a faith of warm, friendly feelings. It's something that stirs their emotions, especially on Sunday, but rarely spurs them to life-changing action. James says what good is a faith of feelings if it has no tangible works to show for itself. If it doesn't work, it's as good as dead!

Now notice the emotional response James anticipates from a hypothetical "someone" who might want to criticize what he's said. Basically, the critic says (verse 18), "Hey, you do faith your way and I'll do it mine," which sounds kind of emotionally defensive to me. And James replies, "Good luck proving your faith without any tangible works to show for it, but as for me, I'm going to prove my faith with action."

Faith certainly involves our emotions, but living, saving faith doesn't stop at feelings. It spurs us to action. It's a faith that mourns over sin, humbly repents, loves unconditionally, forgives repeatedly, and willingly yields in obedience to the Lordship of Jesus Christ. It's life changing. It's a new birth. It's the old life passing away and all things becoming new. That's how God's Word describes saving faith. Is your faith working these things in your life?

Faith is also more than just mental assent. The devil and all his demons believe in God. They know He exists, and they know Jesus Christ is God in the flesh; but they've rebelled against His authority, refused to submit to His will, and hate God. They acknowledge He is God, but they've placed no faith in Him whatsoever. Simply to admit there is a God does not constitute faith in God.

Unfortunately, this is where many people are today, and they don't even know it. They say they believe in God, that they believe in Jesus; but they ignore His Word, resist His will, and fail to give Him any significant priority in their lives. Is that faith? No! It's insanity, because if you really believe in an Almighty God who is your judge and only chance for salvation and heaven, you better listen to what He has to say, you better care what He thinks, you better depend on Him and let Him direct your life. Anything else is a fool's errand. James says if that's what you think faith is, then you are a foolish fellow indeed.

Another evidence of faith is our willingness to make sacrifices. When Abraham believed God's promise to give him an heir and that through him all the world would be blessed, it wasn't just words; it wasn't just a surge of emotion, or just a mental nod of acknowledgement. His faith in God moved him to offer Isaac as a sacrifice with such confidence in God's promise that he fully expected God would raise him from the dead. Abraham's faith had legs. It had meat on its bones. It made him willing to sacrifice the dearest thing he had in life—his son. Of course, God called to stop Abraham because God was looking ahead to the sacrifice of His dear Son, Jesus Christ, to fulfill His promise to Abraham in a way that Isaac's death never could. Yes, Abraham and all of us are saved by faith alone, but what justifies the quality of our faith and proves it as a faith that endures to the saving of the soul is whether or not our faith is willing to make sacrifices. Has your faith caused you to make sacrifices for God?

Finally, faith requires us to take sides. Nobody in Jericho had faith in the God of Israel. They believed themselves safe behind the impenetrable walls of the city. No one except a harlot named Rahab, who chose against her own people to take sides with God and His people. So many people claim to have faith but straddle the line and sit on the fence between God's will and their own. They may jump off for a time, but when the choice to take sides gets hard, they jump right back up on the fence. The persecution of Christians is on the rise today. Believers are being martyred in places like Africa and the Middle East. Even right here in America, believers have been labeled as intolerant and accused of hate speech just for speaking God's truth in love to stand against sin. Will our faith prove worthy to side with Jesus no matter what names we're called, or will we give tacit approval to evil by cowering in silence?

I once read about a man who died, and his two closest friends were at the viewing standing beside the coffin, looking down at his corpse, reminiscing about what a great guy and good friend he was. When they fell silent and were about to leave, one turned to the other and said, "What do you hope people will say about you when you're gone?" The other said, "Well, I hope they look down at me lying in a coffin and say, 'Hey, look. He's still breathing!'"

Friends, is your faith breathing? Can you detect a pulse that beats with God's heart? Does it feel warm to the people your faith touches? When people look at your claim of faith, do they see life or a lifeless corpse? Faith isn't just a mental and emotional claim; it's a lifestyle. It's what we live by and what we are willing to die for.

> For you have need of endurance, so that when you have done the will of God, you may receive what was promised... But we are not of those who shrink back to destruction, but of those who have faith to the preserving of the soul. (Hebrews 10:36, 39)

ROAD RAGE

(JAMES 3:1–12)

R oad rage seems to be an ever-increasing problem these days, and it's likely that most of us have been on the receiving end of some angry driver's curses. Hopefully, as Spirit-filled Christians, we were able to respond with grace rather than retaliate with curses of our own. Unfortunately, stories abound of drivers who have retaliated by setting up a reckless contest of angry and selfish wills that ended in accidents and death.

God reminds us that while the tongue can be used for great good, it can also be used to do great harm. Therefore, He inspires James to write us a very strong warning about our tongue in order to motivate and encourage us to yield our untamable tongue to the taming hand of God.

What we say matters for two reasons. First of all, verse 1 reminds us that our words will be judged. I think we all recognize that teachers, because they provide instruction and exert a great deal of influence over their students, need to be held to a higher standard of speech and conduct. I think this is why so many people have a fear of public speaking. When you stand before a group of people, all eyes and ears are on you, and what you say better be right, because you will be judged by your words and your words have the power to influence your listeners toward truth and righteousness or falsehood and failure.

As one called of God to teach His Word, believe me when I say that I teach in fear and some trembling with the knowledge that God is hanging on my every word, and I will face His stricter judgment for whether I teach His Word correctly or incorrectly. Many, in shaking my hand at the conclusion of a worship service, have mentioned that my hands are so cold, and this is why. I love to preach, but it's a fearful responsibility.

What we say matters, and the fact that James points out it matters even more for those who hold a teaching position does not absolve those who don't teach; that it matters *more* for teachers only highlights that it matters for all of us. Besides, who of us doesn't teach? As we gain experience and seniority in our workplace, we teach and mentor the less experienced. Parents are teachers to their children, and even older siblings teach little brothers and sisters by their words and example. Though relatively few hold formal teaching positions, all of us teach and all of us are accountable to God for what we teach others, especially in regard to our faith and what God's Word declares as right and wrong.

Jesus said, "But I tell you that every careless word that people speak, they shall give an accounting for it in the day of judgment; for by your words you will be justified, and by your words you will be condemned" (Mt.12:36–37). Anybody else's hands getting cold now? Cold hands are fine. It means you take God's Word seriously; just don't have cold feet and not respond to the prompting of the Holy Spirit when he does prompt you to share your faith.

Second, verse 2 says that what we say matters because none of us are without fault. None of us can boast of perfection in our speech, which means that we're all guilty of misusing our tongue. Washington Irving is quoted as saying, "The tongue is the only tool that grows sharper with constant use." He's right, of course, because it seems the more we use our tongue, the more likely we are to misuse it; and we're all guilty of tongue violations.

We lie, we gossip, we insult, we embellish, we flirt, we grumble and complain, we may struggle with profanity, or we tell off color jokes. If we could control our tongue, we could overcome every other wrong in our life, but we can't. Look down to verse 8, which says, "But no one can tame the tongue; it is a restless evil full of deadly poison." Our tongue is our own worst enemy, the first and greatest betrayer of our own lack of self-control.

Some might be tempted to minimize the seriousness of misspoken words by quoting, "Sticks and stones may break my bones, but words will never hurt me," but the truth is that all of us have been hurt by the careless words of others and understand full well the tremendous power of our words. Words have the power of control (verses 3–5). Just as a horse's bridle bit and the rudder of a ship are very small objects in relation to what they control, so the tongue, though a small member of the body, exercises a significance and influence far out of proportion to its size; it "boasts of great things," James says.

The controlling influence of speech is almost beyond imagination. One self-serving word can easily direct a listener down the wrong path. A thoughtless insult, an unfair criticism, a discouraging word, repeating gossip—they can change the course of a whole life and lead a person to discouragement, depression, a tarnished reputation, or even suicide.

On the other hand, a kind, Spirit-led word can direct a soul out of sin and into salvation and out of discouragement and into joy, provide comfort in the midst of grief, and turn self-doubt into confident dependence on God. We can't deny that words have the power to control, so the all-important question is, "Who's in control of our tongue?" We can't trust *ourselves* to always bite our tongue when we should? No! Just as the horse needs someone to hold the reins and the ship needs a pilot on the rudder, so our tongue needs to be yielded to the guiding hand of God.

Hold that thought for a moment and notice that words also have the power to destroy (verses 5–8). James uses three illustrations to emphasize the destructive nature of our tongues.

Fire! Just one untamed spark can set a raging forest fire that destroys thousands of acres, just as one small untamed word can set a friendship, a marriage, a family, a community, or even a whole nation ablaze with anger, bitterness, and hatred. In verse 6, James reminds us of the words of Jesus in Matthew 15:18–20a: "The things that proceed out of the mouth come from the heart, and those defile the man. For out of the heart come evil thoughts, murders, adulteries, fornications, thefts, false witness, slanders. These are the things which defile the man." Destructive words come from a defiled heart and trace back even further to their original source—hell. Fiery, destructive words are the devil's work!

Wild animals! Like the wildest animal, the tongue can't be domesticated. Ironic, isn't it? Man can tame lions and tigers and bears and dolphins and even charm cobras, but we can't tame our own tongue. Why? Because we are all born with a sin nature and our tongue's natural instinct is to be wild. Therefore, none of us have the wisdom or ability to domesticate our tongue and be in full control of our words.

Poison! Whether we mean to or not, no matter how hard we try to bite our tongue and control our speech, we still spout poisonous words that sicken and kill our relationships.

The obvious conclusion is that our tongue is a schizophrenic mess (verses 9–12). With the same tongue, we praise God and wish ill will toward people created in God's image; with it we worship God and curse people Jesus died to save. It doesn't make good sense; it shouldn't be so.

James points out that even nature itself is more consistent than how we use our tongues. A spring always produces the same kind of water and a tree the same kind of fruit, but who knows what the tongue will produce from one moment to the next?

Our tongue is a big problem! Our words matter. God is going to judge our words, and none of us are without fault. Our words have great power to do good or evil, but the truth is none of us can consistently tame our tongue, keep it under control, or use it for good.

It all sounds kind of hopeless, doesn't it? What can we do? The American writer and statesman William Norris said, "If your lips would keep from slips, five things observe with care: To whom you speak; of whom you speak; and how, and when, and where." Well, it makes for a good rhyme and sounds like clever advice, but if the tongue is untamable, it's about as helpful as trying to stop a swarm of bees with a flyswatter. You can try all you want, but you're still going to get stung.

Now God has us right where He wants us. No amount of our own self-control will ever be able to tame our tongue. Tongue control can never come from within or by any human means; it can only come from above. What we can never tame, God can.

We will learn more about "wisdom from above" in the next chapter, but for now, would you agree with God that you need His help? Would you commit to pray for God to tame your tongue?

> Set a guard, O Lord, over my mouth; keep watch
> over the door of my lips. (Psalm 141:3)

Make it your habit to pray: Father God, put Your bit in my mouth and hold the reins of my tongue, that my speech be led by Your indwelling Holy Spirit to be full of blessing and praise that brings honor and glory to You and my Lord and Savior, Jesus Christ. Amen!

SHOCK ABSORBERS

(JAMES 3:13–18)

My '66 VW Bug was in bad need of new shocks. Shortly after buying it, I discovered that if you hit a bump just right, the front end would start to shake and get progressively more severe until you slowed down enough to make it smooth out again. The first time it happened, I just thought it was a bad patch of road; but after the shaking occurred on a couple different roads, I realized it had to be the car. On one occurrence, my granddad happened to be in the car with me, and being a man of quick wit and a keen sense of humor, he started laughing and sarcastically said, "This thing rides pretty good when it's stationary." At the time, I didn't think it was very funny, but the experience did teach me that without good shock absorbers, there's no way your car will have a peaceful ride.

A peaceful ride! Isn't that what all of us hope for in life? We hope that nothing happens to shake up our plans or our confidence and that our trip through life is a relatively smooth one. But as we've already noted, life has its rough patches. The way ahead won't always be a smooth road. So it's just as important for us to have a good set of shock absorbers that help dampen those bumps in the road and give us a smoother ride over them.

James points us to the kind of spiritual shock absorbers we need by asking in James 3:13, "Who among you is wise and understanding?" Think about it. What set of godly virtues could smooth out the bumps and give us peace of mind any better than to have wisdom and understanding for anything and everything we might have to go through?

So to help us answer his question, James goes on to tell us what wisdom and understanding look like where the "rubber meets the road." Christians show themselves to be wise and understanding by demonstrating good behavior and a spirit of gentleness. Consider the following as context.

> See, I have taught you statutes and judgments just as the LORD my God commanded me, that you should do thus in the land where you are entering to possess it. So keep and do *them*, for that is your *wisdom and your understanding* in the sight of the peoples who will hear all these statutes and say, "Surely this great nation is a *wise and understanding* people." (Deuteronomy 4:5–6)
>
> And to man He said, "Behold, the fear of the Lord, that is *wisdom*; And to depart from evil is *understanding*." (Job 28:28)
>
> The fear of the LORD is the beginning of *wisdom*; A good *understanding* have all those who do *His commandments*; His praise endures forever. (Psalm 111:10)

Notice how James 3:13 and all these Old Testament quotes link wisdom and understanding together. Wisdom doesn't just know things, but it also understands them. Most people know right from wrong and have some basic knowledge of the Ten Commandments, but only the truly wise understand that God's Word is never to be ignored but always obeyed. Most people acknowledge there is a God in heaven, but they largely ignore Him. Only the truly wise understand He is to be feared and allow the reality of His judgment to motivate them to avoid evil and embrace good.

A wise and understanding person respects the authority of God's Word and strives to obey it. However, obedience alone is not enough. We can't obey grudgingly, feel miserable about how God's Word cramps our style, and be a "gloomy Gus" because we can't engage in the sins that our unbelieving peers seem to have so much fun doing, or be bitter, judgmental, and holier-than-thou toward those who do. No, our obedience should flow out of a gentle spirit at peace in God's love and full of the true joy of our salvation.

For instance, God's Word says,

> A gentle answer turns away wrath, But a harsh word stirs up anger. (Proverbs 15:1)

> Rejoice in the Lord always; again I will say, rejoice! Let your gentle *spirit* be known to all men. The Lord is near. (Philippians 4:4–5)

> Malign no one, be peaceable, gentle, showing every consideration for all men. (Titus 3:2)

Most people, especially men, equate gentleness with weakness, but let me tell you, being gentle of spirit is hard work. It takes great strength to control your temper, to not be easily provoked or irritated, to bite your tongue, to not get anxious or worried under stress but prayerful, to never insult but show respect and consideration for others in any situation. Unfortunately, *God's wisdom* of good behavior and gentle deeds is not our natural tendency, is it? What does come naturally to us—let's call it the natural "wisdom" we instinctively default to—is the exact opposite of God's wisdom.

So let's compare these two kinds of wisdom. Natural "wisdom" flows out of a selfish, competitive, prideful nature that wants to be first and come out on top over everyone else and resents it when it doesn't get its own way. It's why in an argument we don't seek to understand but just want to win. When hurt, our first impulse is to hurt back; and when others succeed where we don't, rather than take an honest look at how we could've done better, we're tempted to envy the success of others and look for someone else to blame for our own failures.

This selfish character of natural "wisdom" only serves to reveal its source. It's not of God. It's not the leading of the Holy Spirit. It can only come from three places, and they're all bad: earthly or worldly values which are self-serving and materialistic, our own lustful sin nature, or the devil's demonic influence. If you're struggling with bitterness, jealousy, selfishness, and/or pride, you can be convinced it's coming from one or a combination of these three sources.

And notice the results: "disorder and every evil thing." Like what? Conflict, unkind words, hurt feelings, bitterness, holding grudges, depression, vengefulness, hatred, and even murder—it results in a rapidly downward spiral of evil. A life out of control and lost in the self-destructive chaos of sinful feelings and behavior. Doesn't sound so wise, does it?

Contrast this kind of "wisdom" with "the wisdom from above." Obviously, wisdom from above is from God—not of the world, not of our sin nature, not demonic, but heavenly, divine, and sinless wisdom. Its character is sevenfold:

1. *Pure* means without any sinful motives or behavior; it's righteous.
2. *Peaceable* means without any competitiveness, without the desire to compare ourselves with others or feel the need to win over others.
3. *Gentle* refers to the general disposition of the soul. Our Holy God has every right to be stern with us and punish us for our sin, crack the whip when we get out of line; but instead, He is kind and patient and deals with us in the gentleness of His love. The NIV uses the word *considerate*. God can be gentle toward us because He is considerate

of the fact that we are but dust, that our spirit is willing but our flesh is weak. Therefore, we should be considerate enough of the weaknesses and flaws of others to be gentle and kind as well.

4. *Reasonable* is the opposite of being stubborn. We all like to get our own way, don't we? And sometimes we're so stubborn about it our reasons why don't even make sense. It's unreasonable to expect we will always get our way. The NIV translates *reasonable* with the word *submissive* because, unless we want to be a hermit off by our lonesome somewhere, we are going to have to be willing to submit our wants and opinions to others.

5. *Full of mercy and good fruits* means not being quick to draw conclusions, judge, or condemn others for wrongs they've done. It's being willing to give the benefit of the doubt, overlook faults, forgive wrongs, and always be ready to offer help to those in need.

6. *Unwavering* means being impartial, without prejudice in how you view and treat others.

7. *Without hypocrisy* means you have no hidden agenda or you make no attempt to mask who you really are with some phony façade or have any intent to deceive. It's being genuine in the sense that you are who you say you are and that you say what you mean and mean what you say.

Obviously, these are all characteristics of godliness, the fruit of the Spirit demonstrated by those who yield to the Spirit's leading (read Galatians 5:22–26). The word *walk* refers to a measured walk. It's the Greek word used for marching. We are to march in rank and keep step with the Spirit. He gives the command and we fall in. He calls the cadence and we keep in step, and notice the result when we follow wherever He leads.

Remember the results of natural wisdom were conflict, chaos, and evil; but wisdom from above creates a climate where gentle seeds of truth and love and kindness can produce a harvest of righteousness and peace. Jesus said, "Blessed are the gentle, for they shall inherit the earth... Blessed are the merciful, for they shall receive mercy... Blessed are the pure in heart, for they shall see God... Blessed are the peacemakers, for they shall be called sons of God" (Matthew 5:5, 7–9).

"Who among you is wise and understanding?" I hope the answer is obvious to all of us. Only those who embrace the wisdom from above, who march in cadence with the Holy Spirit to lead them to fruits of righteousness and peace.

> The fear of the Lord is the beginning of wisdom, and the knowledge of the Holy one is under-standing. (Proverbs 9:10)

RIGHT-OF-WAY

(JAMES 4:1–7)

When we arrive at an intersection, knowing who has the right-of-way is critical to everyone's safety. The rule states that whoever comes to a stop first gets to go first, and if two cars come to a stop together, then the one on the right goes first. It's a simple rule and works quite well in a polite society, but have you noticed that a lot of people don't seem to care anymore about who has the right-of-way? Unfortunately, many people today have such a self-centered "me first" attitude that they've convinced themselves their rights should come before anyone else's. If someone else's right-of-way gets in their way, then "Look out, I'm coming through" anyway.

Selfishness is dangerous, not just on the road, but in all of life's pursuits. So much so that, here in James 4, God uses words like *quarrels, conflicts, war, lust,* and *murder* to drive home the terrible consequences of self-centered thinking that places personal pleasure above all else. Notice in verse 1 that God says every selfish act springs from our desire for pleasure. The word *pleasures* is the Greek word *hedonon,* from which we get our English word *hedonism.* Hedonism is a philosophy that views pleasure as the chief goal of life. "If it feels good, do it." Practically speaking, it's having the attitude that the most important thing in life is being happy.

Most of our Founding Fathers were godly men, but even they got the purpose of life wrong in the Declaration of Independence. They espoused "life, liberty, and the pursuit of happiness" as the highest ideals of human existence. So now, on top of our own sinful nature to be selfish, we've enshrined as our highest political and social ideals to think in terms of "my life, my liberty, my happiness"—"these are my rights." And this kind of thinking tempts us to be very selfish, self-centered people.

Now, don't get me wrong. I love America and am very grateful for its opportunities for life, liberty, and the pursuit of happiness; but let me ask you, do these ideals agree with what God's Word says? Jesus said, in Luke 9:23–24, "If anyone wishes to come after Me, he must deny himself, and take up his cross daily and follow Me. For whoever wishes to save his life will lose it, but whoever loses his life for My sake, he is the one who will save it." Paul told the Corinthians, "In Christ Jesus our Lord, I die daily."

As a follower of Christ, I must recognize that my life is not really mine. It's God's! He gave me life so I could offer it up as a living sacrifice for His glory rather than my happiness. My flesh tries to exert a declaration of independence that demands "my life, my liberty, and my happiness"; but my faith in Christ encourages me to make a declaration of dependence that emphasizes "life" in Christ, "liberty" from sin to serve God, and the "pursuit" of holiness.

God has not freed us from the power and penalty of sin to spend our liberty for our own self-indulgence or self-promotion. He has given us spiritual and political liberty for the purpose of serving Him and serving others in His name. I've heard people say, "God wants me to be happy, and living with my girlfriend or boyfriend makes me happy, so it must be okay with God." That's blasphemy! God never favors happiness over holiness. There is no "my life, my liberty, my happiness." God has given me life and liberty in order to make me His holy child, and it is only in His will that I will find His "joy unspeakable and full of glory" (1 Peter 1:8).

"As obedient children, do not be conformed to the former lusts *which were yours* in your ignorance, but like the Holy One who called you, be holy yourselves also in all *your* behavior; because it is written, "YOU SHALL BE HOLY, FOR I AM HOLY" (1 Peter 1:14–16). Our heavenly Father's greatest desire for us is not happiness but holiness. It isn't that God doesn't want us to be happy; it's just that He knows that the fullness of joy He's promised will never be found in the pursuit of happiness, but only in the pursuit of holiness.

Brothers and sisters in Christ, is holiness your highest ideal, or is life for you more about your happiness? Notice in verses 1–2 what James is inspired to share about life and liberty spent in the pursuit of happiness; see if this sounds like a happy life to you. First, it makes us green with envy. If life is mostly about what makes you happy, what gives you pleasure and makes you feel good, you will be miserable, because no matter how hard you try, you will never get everything you want. There will always be people out there who have what you don't but think you deserve, and the more you look at what they have that you don't, the more jealous and resentful you will become. "Those evil top 1 percent wage earners, it's not fair that they have so much, and I have so much less." Sound familiar? Envy is not very Christian!

Think about it: every quarrel, conflict, war, or murder that has ever occurred is the result of people not getting their way, what they thought would give them pleasure and make them happy. The selfish pursuit of happiness has caused every single conflict the world has ever seen from a simple argument between friends to mass genocide, from Cain's murder of Abel to today's growth of terrorism. The pursuit of happiness does not make Christians happier people or even the world a happy place.

Notice also that selfishness hinders our prayers. "You do not have because you do not ask. You ask and do not receive because you ask with wrong motives, so that you may spend it on your pleasures." We need to ask ourselves two rather humbling questions:

1. How much of my time and energy is spent on working to get what I want for myself rather than spent in prayer to better discern God's will?

2. When I do pray, how much am I asking for me, myself, and mine (for what I want) versus praying for what God wants, like the progress of the gospel and holding up the needs of others before God?

I have to conclude, at least in my own life, that so many of my worries, frustrations, criticisms, and conflicts with others would be eliminated if I just cared a lot less about having my way and prayed a lot more about God having His way. Perhaps you could draw the same conclusion.

So the slippery slope of self-centered thinking starts with our desire for personal pleasure, but notice where we slide next. Verses 4–5 says it also makes us adulterers. Remember, God is rebuking believers, professing Christians, who seem more concerned about happiness in the world than being holy before Him. Much like in marriage, where having an affair constitutes adultery, God says that when believers are more enamored with the pleasures of the world than the things of God, it's like we're cheating on Him, being unfaithful, having an affair; we are committing adultery against God.

After all, what's the church, to which all believers belong, called? The Bride of Christ! Obviously, adultery is no small thing in any marriage. In how many marriages has adultery turned a loving couple into enemies? James says even more so with God, because God is a jealous husband! God has married us. He has chosen to share His eternal life with us, and he has moved into our souls in the person of His Holy Spirit to intimately dwell within us. Like any good spouse would be, in the most appropriate sense of jealousy, God has no desire to share us with another lover. He doesn't want us sleeping around with worldly pleasures.

Listen to what Paul wrote to the very worldly church in Corinth. As the one who shared the gospel and brought the Corinthians to Christ, Paul likens himself to a minister who officiated their wedding with God, and he says, "For I am jealous for you with a godly jealousy; for I betrothed you to one husband, so that to Christ I might present you *as* a pure virgin. But I am afraid that, as the serpent deceived Eve by his craftiness, your minds will be led astray from the simplicity and purity *of devotion* to Christ" (2 Corinthians 11:2–3). God is jealous for our holiness, which brings us to the bottom-line tragedy of putting the pursuit of happiness over the pursuit of holiness.

To put happiness before holiness is to believe the devil's lie. What lie is that? The lie he told Eve in the garden of Eden and the same lie he's been telling ever since. "Eat the fruit. It will make you wise and you'll see that you don't need God. You can be your own god and have what you want and do what you want whenever you want." He appealed to her pride and pride's selfish desire for personal pleasure. You see, when we place happiness over holiness, we play right into the devil's hand, a place we definitely don't want to be! And a place we don't have to be because the devil is resistible with God's help.

God gives a greater grace! Yes, God's standards are high. He wants our wholehearted faithfulness and our commitment to holiness, and we all sometimes stray into affairs with the world and put our own happiness first. "But where sin increased, grace abounded all the more, so that, as sin reigned in death, even so grace would reign through righteousness to eternal life through Jesus Christ our Lord" (Romans 5:20–21).

God's grace is greater than all our sin. When we humbly confess our sins, He showers us with the grace of His forgiveness. When we swallow our pride, He pours on more grace. When we submit our happiness to His holiness, we receive yet more grace to resist even the devil's biggest lie; and when we finally leave this world, God's grace will carry us to His eternal home.

> As obedient children, do not conform to the evil desires you had when you lived in ignorance. But just as he who called you is holy, so be holy in all you do; for it is written: "Be holy, because I am holy." (1 Peter 1:14–16)

DRIVING STRESSES (PART 1)

(JAMES 4:6–8A)

Several years ago, Tracie and I were driving back from visiting some of her cousins in Louisiana to Yuma, Arizona, where I was stationed as the command chaplain for Marine Corps Air Station Yuma. Our visit had been wonderful, and the trip was going smoothly, until as darkness set in over west Texas, we saw a great deal of lightning ahead and knew we were driving into a thunderstorm.

If you've ever driven across west Texas, you know that towns are few and far between; so since there was no place to stop, we pressed on into the storm, hoping it would only amount to a quick downpour. Boy, were we wrong! I've never seen it rain so hard in my life; even with the wipers going full blast and slowing from an eighty-miles-per-hour speed limit to just creeping along, I was hardly able to see well enough to stay in my lane. If that wasn't bad enough, the rain gave way to quarter-sized hail, so severe that I thought the windshield would break and feared we might be driving into a tornado without even knowing it.

Talk about a white-knuckle grip on the wheel. I've been in combat with infantry Marines in Iraq but can truly say that I've never been more scared than driving through that storm, nor have I ever breathed a greater sigh of relief than when we finally drove through it. When we were finally to civilization and able to exit the interstate, we discovered what turned out to be over $6000 of hail damage to our car.

Just as driving through storms can add a lot of stress to a road trip, so can the many responsibilities of our faith. Think of the spiritual road trip we've been on so far. God's standard of holiness is no small feat, and James pulls no punches in chastising us for all the things we've been doing wrong.

We're supposed to rejoice in trials. "Come on. Can't I complain a little?" When we're tempted and fall into sin, we can't blame anyone but ourselves? "Gee, thanks, James, as if I don't already feel bad enough." We're not just encouraged to read the Bible, but God actually expects us to know what it means and practice it. "What? Are you kidding me?" It isn't enough to just treat certain people with care and respect, but we're supposed to love everyone without prejudice. "Seriously?" We can't just say we believe in God and we love Jesus, but we should offer evidence of our faith in how we live? "What's up with that?" And if all this weren't enough, James has the audacity to tell us we all have potty mouths none of us can fully control. "Shut up!" James's point exactly! And finally, imagine now, James actually calls us adulterers just because sometimes we put our own happiness ahead of holiness. "Man, can't we have any fun?"

Well, this is just great! Encourage me some more, James. Ever felt like that, even just a little? The truth is that salvation by faith is easy, incredibly easy; all you have to do is believe and receive it as a free gift. But living by faith is hard! You think the military expects a lot. Let me tell you: living out an "I really mean it with all my heart" faith makes boot camp look like summer camp.

After laying out all these rigorous demands of living by faith, I think God knew we would be feeling a bit stressed, if not overwhelmed, and perhaps need a little intermission from His spiritual boot camp. So in the middle of chapter 4, James pauses to give us a sigh of relief, a chance to catch our breath and take a deep, refreshing breath of God's amazing grace.

We touched on it in James 4:6–7, where it says that God "gives a greater grace" to the humble who submit to Him and resist the devil. So let's pick up there and look in verses 8–10 at the first of four deep breaths of God's grace. First, God's grace allows us to enjoy closeness with Him. "Draw near to God and he will draw near to you" (James 4:8). This is one of the greatest statements of the Bible. It means that God wants us to be close to Him. He wants to have a relationship with us so much more than just Creator and creature or judge and the one to be judged. No, He wants to be a Father to us, "Our Father, Who art in heaven," we pray. Even more, He wants to be our closest friend. Jesus said, "Greater love has no one than this, that one lay down his life for his friends... I have called you friends, for all things that I have heard from My Father I have made known to you" (John. 15:13, 15). God wants to bring us into His good graces and have the kind of close friendship with us where secrets are shared and everything is talked about. He wants to be our BFF, literally.

God wants to be close to us, but the longer I live and the more I draw near to God, the more I am absolutely convinced that we are all only as close to God as we want to be. God doesn't limit our closeness with Him; we do. So we all need to consider two questions:

1. How close to God do I really want to be? Friendship is a conditional relationship. In order to have friends, we have to reach out, be friendly, and make friends with people who choose to receive our friendship. God wants to be our friend and has proven it by taking the initiative to reach out to us in Jesus Christ. Jesus said, "I am the way, the truth, and the life; no one can come to the Father but by Me" (John 14:6). So in order to enjoy friendship with God, we must first choose to acknowledge Jesus Christ as Lord and Savior and believe in His death, burial, and resurrection as the only sacrifice worthy to pay for our sin. We can't save ourselves; only Jesus can. Ephesians 2:13 says, "But now

in Christ Jesus you who formerly were far off [from God] have been brought near by the blood of Christ."

Trusting Christ begins our friendship with God, but how close will the friendship be? Do you just want to be casual friends, just a friend when you need something from God, a close friend; or would you want God to be your best friend? How close we want to be to God is not just up to God but also how close we want to be to Him. "Draw near to God and He will draw near to you" (James 4:8). Which brings us the next question:

2. How can I draw near? Well, how do we draw near to any friend? What does it take for an acquaintance to become a friend and for the friendship to grow closer? We have to spend time together, talk to one another, discover some shared interests, lower our guard and be willing to let this person see who we really are, and see if they have the grace to love us as we are and us them. Friendships don't happen automatically. They take an investment of time and self and grace for closeness to occur.

An hour on Sunday morning won't do it. Being less than honest and trying to hold back what you really think and how you feel only builds walls. You know, I think we hold back drawing near to God because we're afraid He will disapprove of us, judge us, punish us for our sin; but the truth is that He's promised to always show us grace.

Ironically, the more we distance ourselves from God, the more we deprive ourselves of the acceptance and love of His grace and the more unworthy we will feel. But the more we draw near to God, no matter how unworthy we feel, the more we will experience the acceptance and love of His grace. Don't wall yourself off from God's grace. His grace is what we all need most. Draw near; desire closeness. For the closer you draw near to God, the more you will know His grace.

Where sin abounds, grace abounds all the more.
(Romans 5:20)

DRIVING STRESSES (PART 2)

(James 4:8b–10)

Exiting that terrible west Texas storm certainly relieved a great deal of our stress, but that $6000 worth of hail damage still ended up creating additional stress down the road. In order to repair the damage, much of the car had to be disassembled to replace whole body panels rather than just pop out dents; and apparently, some wiring or electrical components must've been damaged during reassembly. Unfortunately, we started to experience strange and intermittent electrical problems, which made the car unreliable and left us with a real concern that the car might leave one of us stranded. Having lost faith in the vehicle, we finally just replaced it and breathed a sigh of relief that we again had a car we could count on.

Fortunately, we can always breathe a sigh of relief in drawing near to the God in whom we need never lose faith because He is absolutely and eternally reliable. "Jesus Christ is the same yesterday and today and forever" (Hebrews 13:8).

In the last chapter, we looked at the first of four deep breaths of God's grace, that God's grace allows us to draw as close to Him as we want to be, and the closer we draw near to Him, the closer He draws near to us. The next deep breath of God's grace is that when we draw near to God, we are cleansed. Our hands are instruments of action (behavior), and the heart an instrument of thoughts and desires. And the idea in verse 8 is that even as Christians who've drawn near to God through faith in Jesus Christ, we still struggle with sinful behavior (we're still sinners) and our thoughts are still sometimes torn between the sinful desires of this world and the desire for God (we're double-minded). Yes, we're saved, but we still need cleansing from our daily sins.

But we can't cleanse ourselves. We might be tempted to read this as something we have to do for ourselves as if James is saying, "Go clean up your act, you naughty, double-minded sinner." But no, only God can accomplish our cleansing for salvation, and only God can wash away the sins we commit as His children. First John 1:9 says, "If we confess our sins, He [Jesus] is faithful and righteous to forgive us our sins and to cleanse us from all unrighteousness." As the old hymn says, "What can wash away my sins? Nothing but the blood of Jesus."

We need to draw near. If we don't draw near to God to confess our sins, we can't get fully clean. God's grace invites us to come to Him in all the filthiness of our sin so His grace can wash it all away and make us feel as pure as God sees us in all the righteousness of Jesus Christ. Don't ever let your sin keep you from drawing near to God. Staying away from God because you feel too sinful to approach Him is like staying away from water because you feel too dirty to take a shower. Hello! Doesn't make sense, does it?

God's grace always invites us to come to Him for cleansing. No matter how many or how bad our sins, when we confess them to Him, He forgives and cleanses us from all unrighteousness. Are you breathing any easier yet? I hope so, but if not, notice another benefit of God's grace to help us breathe easier.

Third, His grace allows us to connect with His heart (verse 9). You might ask, "How is mourning and weeping a refreshing breath of

God's grace?" Well, let's think about the heart of God for a moment. God is brokenhearted over sin's invasion and infection of His perfect creation. He weeps over the damage it has done. Jesus did not weep at the tomb of Lazarus because He was mourning the loss of a friend. He knew He would raise him from the dead in a few moments. No, He wept over the suffering and sorrow and death that sin had brought into the world and into our lives. Jesus wept over Jerusalem because sin had so blinded the eyes of His people that they couldn't see and accept Him as their Savior. Sin makes God sad. It brings tears to His eyes. It is His heart to mourn over how sin has painted its ugly graffiti all over His masterpiece of creation.

Friends, the closer we draw near to God and the more immersed in His grace we become, the more we will be connected with His heart to mourn over sin like He mourns over sin. Think of how enlightening and how liberating it is to view sin as God does, as something to mourn and weep over. It would cease to be a temptation. Who is tempted to go to a funeral? Who is tempted to run toward sadness? These are things to be avoided if at all possible; and so sin should be, and will be, the more our hearts become connected with God's heart. The more deeply we breathe in God's grace, the easier it is for us to walk in the refreshing liberty of the Holy Spirit's leading.

Finally, the fourth deep breath of God's grace brings with it His commendation. In the military, we're familiar with commendations. If we do a good job, we may receive a Letter of Commendation, maybe even a Navy Marine Corps Commendation Medal. It's nice to have that approval and recognition of service above and beyond the call of duty. But wouldn't you agree it would be so much better to know we have God's approval, to receive God's commendation of "Well-done, my good and faithful servant"?

We tend to relate this hope to heaven, but we don't have to wait until heaven to know God's approval. We have God's promise that every time we humbly come into His presence, we will have His approval, that just coming to Him is reason enough for Him to exalt or lift us up.

Romans 8:1 proclaims, "Therefore there is now *no condemnation* for those who are in Christ Jesus," which means the only thing left is His loving acceptance. God always extends His hand of approval to His children. "You are my child. I love you. I'm so glad you've come. I'm so proud of you." This is what we always have to look forward to when we breathe deeply of God's grace. God's grace promises closeness, cleansing, connection, and commendation. How can we refuse? How can we stay away? Why hold your breath when you can breathe so deeply of God's grace?

> Therefore, the Lord longs to be gracious to you, And therefore He waits on high to have compassion on you. For the Lord is a God of justice; How blessed are all those who long for Him. (Isaiah 30:18)

> Let everything that has breath praise the Lord. Praise the Lord! (Psalm 150:6)

DON'T PLAY CHICKEN

(JAMES 4:11–17)

There is much in the news these days about self-driving cars. Many in the auto industry are heralding this advancement in technology as the wave of the future and even predicting the end of the need of a steering wheel within the next twenty years, if not sooner. To prove the viability and reliability of self-driving cars, some auto industry executives have bravely, or perhaps foolishly, put their lives on the line to test this technology by jumping out in front or running toward these cars, confident that their car will detect the hazard and safely stop in time.

It was in the news just the other day that a pedestrian was killed by a self-driving car, so I think it's safe to say that it would be foolish to risk your life on the assumption that everything will work as planned. Autonomous cars aren't perfect. They get into fender benders, have trouble navigating in bad weather, and have been known to run red lights. Yes, the technology is constantly improving, but to assume it is safe to play chicken with a car designed and built by fallible human beings is, well, foolish.

I'll tell you what's even more foolish, and that's trying to play chicken with God. How is that even possible? To play chicken is to challenge another to a contest of will and nerve to see who backs down first. It suggests at least the possibility of victory for either contestant or at least equality if both back down at the same time. In the case of playing chicken with God, it betrays an arrogant belief that we are just as much in charge of things as God is, and we may even have a chance to best Him, which is, in effect, playing God ourselves. "Who would ever dare to play God?" you ask. Unfortunately, the answer is, all of us. As a matter of fact, James 4:11–17 points out two ways we all commonly try to play God.

Notice first that we dare to play God when we judge others. James uses two words to describe the judgmental kind of attitude God warns against. The first word is translated as "speak against." It refers to any speech that is malicious in nature, speech that tears down a person in some way rather than building them up. It's a word that was actually used to refer to a dog nipping at someone's heel as they walked along, so it came to be used of backbiting speech, things like gossip, slander, criticism spoken behind a person's back that create a negative impression or even reputation that follows them and nips at their heels wherever they go. "Oh, here comes Slater. So-and-so told me that he's a real piece of work."

"Hey," God says, "who gave you the right to talk Slater down or help spread negative rumors about him?" We've all had it done to us, right? And it's no fun. The truth is we all make enough mistakes of our own, and we don't need anybody else's help to fuel the grapevine; so we shouldn't do it to others. Ephesians 4:29 says, "Let no unwholesome word proceed from your mouth, but only such *a word* as is good for edification according to the need *of the moment,* so that it will give grace to those who hear."

Now, not all judgment is wrong; actually, it's very necessary. Jesus said in John 7:24, "Do not judge according to appearance, but judge with righteous judgment." Using the standard of God's Word to know what is right or wrong, true or false, we are commanded to judge behavior as righteous or sinful. Lying is a sin! Adultery is a sin! Not because I said so, but because God said so. We have to make judgments every day to avoid what is evil and cling to what is good, to embrace what is true and reject what is false. When we agree with God that His Word is true and His judgments are just and good and right, we are judging with righteous judgment. But judgment we should not do, that we have no right to make, is to judge the person, their motives, their heart, or the destiny of their soul.

It's one thing to catch a person in a lie and say, "You lied." That is a righteous judgment in agreement with God's Word, which says, "Thou shalt not bear false witness." But that doesn't give us the right to say, "Because you lied, you are a horrible person. You obviously don't care about the truth. Nobody should ever trust you again. You must not be a Christian. You are going to hell."

Whoa! Do you see how that's crossing a line? We can't know their heart. We can't know their true motives. We have no right to absolve or condemn a person's soul. Only God knows our hearts and our faith, and only God can save, and only God can condemn. So we should never make the kind of judgments that cause us to speak against others or judge anything about a person other than whether their behavior is right or wrong according to the standard of God's Word. We should never judge based on our own opinion, and any righteous judgment we must make should always be done with love and concern for the person, to help them, not hurt them, and with humble understanding that we have plenty of faults ourselves. "Brethren, even if anyone is caught in any trespass, you who are spiritual, restore such a one in a spirit of gentleness; *each one* looking to yourself, so that you too will not be tempted" (Galatians 6:1).

James shares three reasons why unrighteous judgment is so evil, and the first is because we are a family (verses 11–12). Remember that James is writing to Christians (brethren) and referring to our relationships with one another as brothers and sisters in the family of God. Yeah, I know there is sibling rivalry in every family, but in a healthy family, it's pretty good-natured most of the time; and after all is said and done, we love each other and protect each other. It's family!

Well, we are the family of God, and sure, we have our differences; and as in every family, there is a need for discipline and accountability for wrongs done, but we should never tear each other down for mistakes or sins committed. We should lovingly correct, forgive, restore, and encourage them to do better, but never speak against or harshly judge our own family. "Who are you to judge your neighbor?" is an obvious reference to our obligation to love our neighbor as ourselves, so all the more our own family.

Second, we must remember that none of us are above the law. Jesus said, "Let him who is without sin cast the first stone." Love is the fulfillment of the law. "Love the Lord your God with all your heart, and with all your soul, and with all your strength, and love your neighbor as yourself." As believers, we are all under, and obligated to obey, the law of love, and we are all guilty of breaking it; so who of us is qualified to be the moral policeman for the rest of us? Nobody!

Third, the judgment of souls belongs only to God. Who *is* above the law? God! Who *is* the ultimate expression and embodiment of love? God! Who *is* the only One qualified to judge the obedience of our faith and love? God! When we love one another, we are apples that don't fall far from the tree; we are acting like God's sons and daughters. When we talk down and judge one another, we dare to play God.

The second way we dare to play God is when we presume on the future. How do we do that? We do it by making plans without God. Notice what a well-laid-out plan these Christian businessmen had in verses 13–16. The starting time was arranged "today or tomorrow." Their destination was chosen to be "such and such a city." The duration of their trip was set "a year" out, and it was just assumed "they would engage in business and make a profit."

In 1785, a Scottish poet named Robert Burns was plowing some ground and overturned a mouse's nest. Burns felt so bad that he had ruined the nest the mouse had built for shelter from the coming winter that he composed the poem from which we get the phrase "The best-laid plans of mice and men often go awry." Have you ever had a plan go wrong?

Now, God isn't condemning good planning. Quite the contrary, Jesus even told a parable about counting the cost of a project before it begins, lest we begin to build and find out we don't have the resources to complete it. What God is denouncing, however, is leaving Him and consideration of His will out of our plans. You see, in their own human ingenuity and arrogant self-sufficiency, these businessmen were charting their own course, planning their own destiny, and trying to dictate their own desired outcome without any thought of God whatsoever.

I went to a buffet restaurant once that had a big sign at the front of the serving line that said, "Life is uncertain. Eat dessert first!" Amen! I love it! Preach it, brother! Likewise, James is reminding us that because life is uncertain and so much of it is out of our control, we should think of God first because He is in control! Proverbs 16:1–3 says, "The plans of the heart belong to man, but the answer of the tongue is from the LORD. All the ways of a man are clean in his own sight, but the LORD weighs the motives. Commit your works to the LORD, And your plans will be established."

By all means, make plans, but bathe them in prayer with an ear tuned to listen to the guidance of the Holy Spirit. Whether planning your career, your family, or even your vacation, don't just try to fit God into your plan. God fills the heavens, and we can't fit Him into anything! We need to always remember that God rules over our plans, so we best get His input.

None of us would consciously think of playing chicken with God or intentionally try to play God, but perhaps all of us have unknowingly done so by judging others and presuming on our own plans for the future; so James sums up with a strong warning in verse 17. "Therefore, to one who knows *the* right thing to do and does not do it, to him it is sin." Perhaps we didn't know any better before. We didn't realize we were playing God in these ways and could plead ignorance, but now that we do know, we have no excuse. You see, with knowledge always comes increased responsibility; and now that we know the truth, we dare not play God.

> Is there any God besides Me, or is there any other
> Rock? I know of none. (Isaiah 44:8b)

BELLS AND WHISTLES

(JAMES 5:1–6)

I remember my dad telling me about how cars were so simple and basic when he was young. As Henry Ford is quoted as saying, "You could have any color you wanted as long as it was black," and any feature other than what was absolutely essential for basic transportation was considered a luxury. Even a heater was an option that cost extra. When I started driving, you could still buy a stripped-down car with no so-called bells and whistles equipped with a three-on-the-tree manual transmission, crank-operated windows, and push-button door locks. Many people opted for these plain-Jane models because they simply couldn't afford all the other options considered unnecessary luxuries at the time.

My how things have changed! Now even the cheapest base model of just about any make of car comes with A/C, a stereo system with Bluetooth technology, power windows and door locks, USB ports, trip odometers, and the all-essential cup holder for the driver and every passenger. Even just one package upgrade can typically add such goodies as heated seats, leather upholstery, a navigation system, power adjustable mirrors, trip computers, backup cameras, and remote starting. All these features and many more are now mostly considered essentials rather than luxuries, and no one wants a stripped-down plain-Jane car anymore.

We welcome the prosperity that has brought on these changes and call it a blessing, and in many ways it is; but with wealth also comes the blurring of the lines between what is truly essential and what is a luxury, and it can blind us to those things in life that are most important. Jesus said that we can't serve two masters. We can't serve God and wealth at the same time, and James 5:1–6 warns all of us about how quickly wealth can turn our hearts away from what faith in Jesus Christ is all about.

The first warning is that wealth can actually be a curse that leads to much weeping and wailing. Ask the majority of big lottery winners whose lives and families were ruined by their instant wealth. The money they thought would solve all their problems and make their life better made them targets of scammers, caused them to be hounded by family and friends looking for handouts, in most cases led to lavish spending, and even in some cases ended in moral decay and bankruptcy.

You might almost be thinking, *Boy, I'm glad I'm not wealthy because I'm not sure I could handle it wisely either.* Well, did you know that global median income is less than $10,000 a year? According to the US Census Bureau, median annual income in the United States was $61,937 in 2018, and even if, as a family of four, you only earn at the US poverty line of about $25,000 a year, it still means you make two and a half times more than the rest of the world.

Are we rich? Absolutely! Filthy rich, as they say, when compared with most of the rest of the world. So how well do we manage our wealth? Are we more dependent on our bank account balance than we are on God to supply our needs? Do we give generously and cheerfully to minister to the less fortunate in Jesus's name, or are we living even beyond our means and amassing debt to reach for an even higher standard of living?

When we consider that Jesus said, "From everyone who has been given much, much will be required; and to whom they entrusted much, of him they will ask all the more" (Luke 12:48), then we must also consider that mishandled wealth can indeed be a curse. To whom much is given, much is expected, so let's look at four what not to dos of wealth:

1. Don't hoard (verse 2–3). The whole purpose of wealth is not to let it sit idle but to use it. Yes, we should have some savings like an emergency fund in case an unexpected expense arises, and yes, we should be prudent to save and invest for our retirement years when we're too old to work. But beyond that, whatever excess we have after we pay the bills should not be hoarded away for our own comfort, luxury, or sense of security but spent for the glory of God.

   Jesus's parable of the rich fool in Luke 12:13–21 ought to be a sufficient reminder of how foolish it is to store up what you can't take with you. James's reference to the "last days" is an added reminder that a judgment day is coming when all of us will answer to God for our stewardship of His money—yeah, His money, not ours. Will God's judgment reveal that we spent his blessings on ourselves, accumulating stuff that wears out and rots away and one day will burn up with the world, or did we store up our treasure in heaven by spending it to spread the gospel and minister to people's needs in Jesus's name? Don't hoard!

2. The next what not to do of wealth is to not gain wealth dishonestly (verse 4). This is a rebuke of the rich who withheld wages due to workers. Perhaps, for example, instead of paying them on payday as expected and needed, they delayed paying them to a later time. Or they promised a certain wage, and when it came time to pay, they made some excuse for why they could only pay a lesser wage. Whatever the means, the wealthy had their ways of dishonestly padding their own wallets on the backs of their workers.

   Unless we run a business and pay employees, we may be tempted to dismiss this as not applying to us, but there are many other ways we can be tempted to gain wealth dishonestly. Do we put in a full day's work for a full day's pay? Do we take any shortcuts in paying our taxes? Do we pay our bills on time or hold back money we should use to pay our debts to spend on our own wants instead? Do we hide money from our spouse to buy stuff without them knowing it rather than stick to the family budget? Do we hold back on our charitable giving so we can afford a nicer house or car? The fact is, the more we have, the more we want, and the desire for wealth and the stuff it can buy can be a powerful temptation to grow dishonest in the drive to get ahead.

3. The third what not to do is to not live lavishly (verse 5). We can all look at the lifestyles of the rich and famous for example after example of living in the lap of extreme luxury. Megamillion-dollar estates, private jets, yachts with helicopters on the deck, ladies who spend $100K for a dress they'll only wear once to some super swanky celebrity-studded event. These are things beyond what most of us would even dream about, let alone be able to do, but you don't have to be a millionaire to live too lavishly.

I can't tell you what living lavishly looks like for you. I have enough struggles of my own trying to be a good steward of what God gives me, so I'm certainly no judge of anyone else.

However, I know that, for me, I don't need a Mercedes when a Subaru will get me where I need to go just as well. I don't need to buy $100 pair of jeans at Macy's when $20 Rustlers from Walmart will do. And if I eat out at all, I'm perfectly content with a pizza from Papa Murphy's we take home to cook than to go to some ritzy restaurant that charges too much for portions too small. And even when I enjoy these lesser options, I have to remain conscious that even these are way beyond the reach, and even the dreams, of more than 80 percent of the rest of the world.

All I can say to you is to listen to that still small voice of the Holy Spirit working in your conscience. When it's time to decide what's a need or a want, what is a reasonable indulgence and what is a luxury that just can't be justified, pray about it; and ask God to restrain you if it's too extravagant or give you peace of mind to whip out the credit card.

Here's a verse that helps me. It's written in the context of whether to eat meat that might have been offered to idols or just to eat vegetables, but the principle really applies to any decision we have to make about anything. Romans 14:23 says, "But he who doubts is condemned if he eats, because *his eating is* not from faith; and whatever is not from faith is sin." This might ruin your whole day, but I'm going to say it anyway. If you can't do something with a completely clear conscience, if you're not sure if it's right or wrong, if you have any doubts, then don't do it! See, we love to play the "gray area" game, don't we? But this totally removes that excuse. For the devoted Christian, there are no gray areas because if we have doubts, our answer must be no! "Whatsoever is not from faith is sin."

4. Finally, don't use your wealth to mistreat others (verse 6). James points to the wealthy of his day who oppressed the poor even to the point of death, and the poor were helpless to defend against it. Under the Roman law of the time, if you owed a debt you couldn't pay, your lender could confiscate all your property and leave you homeless, sell you into slavery, or send you to a debtors' prison—any of which could be as good as a death sentence. To put it into some perspective for us today, it would be like a millionaire insisting on a life sentence at hard labor for a poor guy who couldn't pay a $1000 debt. Hardly fair, but legal under Roman law. And this was happening to poor first-century Christians at the hand of the rich, in some cases, even at the hands of wealthy people who also professed to be Christians. "Nothing personal, brother, it's just business."

Now, we can't just dismiss this as not applying to us today because our laws protect the poor from this kind of injustice. If we brag about what we have to someone with less, have we mistreated them? Yes! If, in our abundance, we withhold help from someone in need, have we mistreated them? Yes! If we use our wealth and influence to somehow hinder someone else from also obtaining what we have, have we mistreated them? Yes!

Much like with our speech, which should only be used to build people up, not tear them down, so it should be with how we use our wealth. As wealthy Christians (remember that even those at the poverty line in America make much more than most people in the world), our privileged position should never be used to demean or deny those who have less but to encourage, inspire, help, and build them up.

Wealth can be a curse. Nothing can lead us away from God quicker than prosperity; so don't hoard your wealth, but invest it for the glory of God. Don't compromise your integrity to try to get ahead, but be honest in all your dealings. Don't live lavishly, but be lavishly generous. Don't be puffed up with pride about what you have, but humble yourself to lift others up. This is what being a good steward of God's blessings is about. He has entrusted all of us with great wealth. Will we use it wisely?

> For the love of money is a root of all sorts of evil,
> and some by longing for it have wandered away
> from the faith and pierced themselves with many
> griefs. (1 Timothy 6:10)

EXPECT DELAYS

(JAMES 5:7–12)

I came upon this sign again just the other day: "Flagman Ahead! Expect Delays!" You have no idea how much I hate those signs. I'd like to think that in many areas of my life, I have learned some measure of patience, but when it comes to driving, I can assure you that I am not a patient person. I have come to realize that because I am a very punctual person and refuse to be late, I always feel like I need to be in a hurry. Even when I leave far too early and tell myself I have plenty of time to just "mosey along," in just a few easygoing miles, I revert to feeling in a hurry and pick up the pace. The irony is that I'll arrive at an appointment even earlier than normal and have to wait that much longer at my destination. I well understand the fellow who first said, "The hurrier I am, the behinder I get."

We somewhat tritely say that "patience is a virtue." We quote clichés like "Good things come to those who wait," and while it's all true, the fact remains that patience is among the most difficult things in life to master, especially in this hurry-up world that we live in. Patience is essential to good character, but it's definitely easier said than done. In James 5:7, it says, "Be patient." It's not a suggestion. It's not optional. It's a command, an order from our supreme commander in heaven that is to be obeyed. Therefore, we all need to slow down and take a careful look at the what, why, and how of following our Lord's command to be patient people.

What is patience? The word refers to having a mind to wait, to not quickly rush ahead but to restrain ourselves from impulsively taking matters into our own hands, which is what we tend to do in life. James illustrates patience with the farmer. In the Israel of James's day, they planted in the fall and harvested in the spring to avoid the scorching heat of summer. The early rains came in October–November soon after the seed was sown, and the later rains came in April–May to mature the crops for harvest. So the farmer had to wait patiently to time his planting and harvesting with the rains. If he planted too early, the seed would sprout and die before the rains came. If the spring rains failed to come, he would get a poor harvest. Yes, he had to do his part to prepare the ground, plant the seed, and cultivate out the weeds; but the final outcome was all in God's hands to provide the right amount of rain at the right time to ensure a good harvest. After his work was done, all he could do was wait on God.

What's true about farming is true in many other areas of life. Whether it's seeking revenge for a wrong done to us rather than waiting on God to judge (vengeance is mine, says the Lord), or making plans without waiting for God's leading, or giving into passion in a relationship rather than keeping the relationship pure until marriage, we should wait on God. Whenever my grandpa Slater would look down at the speedometer and catch himself speeding, he would let off the gas and say, "Hold'r Newt, she's headed for the silo!" He remembered the days of horse and wagon when the horse would pick up speed as it got close to home, and you'd have to pull back on the reins to slow the horse down. That's what we need to do. When we are tempted to rush ahead of God, take matters into our own hands, and bull our own way through, patience is having the ability to rein ourselves in, throttle back, and wait on God. But why?

Notice in verses 7–9 the phrases "until the coming of the Lord… for the coming of the Lord is near…the Judge is standing right at the door." Three times we are reminded that God is in control. He is orchestrating our lives and the whole world according to His plan. Every experience, interruption, annoyance, success, or failure in our lives, our country, and the world that challenges our patience is all part of God's plan to shape our character and prepare his people for eternal joy in heaven and, of course, judge the unbelieving world. The point is, do we trust God to carry out His plan?

This is why it is so important that we be patient. Patience is an expression of our trust and dependence on God. Impatience is an expression of our lack of faith that God knows what He's doing, so we try to rush ahead and take control of life ourselves. This reminds us that no matter how good or bad life is, no matter how we feel about the direction our country is going or how screwed up the world is, is God in control? Yes! Is Jesus coming again to redeem His people, judge the world, and claim His rightful place as King of kings and Lord of lords? Yes! Then be patient. Trust that God will work His good will and pleasure in your life. He will do away with sin, and He will reign in righteousness forever; and we will reign with Him. The coming of the Lord is near. The judge is standing right at the door. So that brings us to how.

How are we to be patient? The first step is by not complaining. The word *complain* literally means to grumble, groan, or sigh. It doesn't refer so much to loud and open complaining, which is bad enough because nobody likes to be around a constant complainer, but it refers more to inner distress that comes from unexpressed feelings of bitterness or smoldering resentment inside that may be expressed with a groan or a sigh. James already warned us back in James 4:6, "God is opposed to the proud but He gives grace to the humble." Believers who have a confident faith in God trust that He is in control and know that He's promised to work all things for good to those who love Him. They receive grace and love from God that enables them to be patient when the world wrongs them or fellow believers irritate them in some way.

However, believers who impatiently complain instead of trusting God will be judged for their complaining. Listen to Philippians 2:13–15:

> For it is God who is at work in you, both to will and to work for *His* good pleasure. Do all things without grumbling or disputing; so that you will prove yourselves to be blameless and innocent, children of God above reproach in the midst of a crooked and perverse generation, among whom you appear as lights in the world.

You see, when we grumble and complain, we just act like the crooked and perverse generation we live in; but when we patiently accept God's work in our lives without grumbling and complaining, we prove ourselves to be children of God letting our light shine for Jesus Christ. So which do you want to be?

The next way we can demonstrate patience is to follow good examples. *Enoch* walked with God for 365 years before God walked him directly to heaven without ever dying. *Noah* labored over 100 years building the ark before the flood came. *Moses* had to spend 40 years in the wilderness tending sheep before God called him to lead Israel out of Egypt. *David* was anointed as king when just a young teen but had to run for his life from King Saul and didn't wear the crown until he was thirty. Jesus, the Son of God and our Lord and Savior, has been in heaven for almost 2000 years, waiting for God the Father to give Him the go-ahead to claim His bride, the church, and assume His rightful place as King of kings and Lord of lords.

Do you kind of start to see a pattern here? It isn't that God gets some kind of perverse pleasure out of making us wait and keeping us in painful suspense. No, there is so much value in waiting we could never receive if we realized God's promises quickly. Did God keep his promises to all these patriarchs, prophets, and kings? After all the waiting, did it turn out exactly as our compassionate and merciful God said it would? Yes! Absolutely! From seeing them wait, and having to wait ourselves, we learn endurance. We gain valuable experience that sets us up for success. Waiting tests our faith and proves it to be genuine and "enduring to the saving of the soul" (Hebrews 10:39). Don't complain.

Third, be faithful to the truth. Christians are to hold such a high degree of honesty and integrity in all our dealings that swearing an oath or having to make a promise is unnecessary because we have the reputation that our word is our bond; we always speak the truth, we do what we say, and we keep our commitments. Billy Joel had a hit song titled "Honesty." In the song he laments, "Honesty, it's such a lonely word. Everyone is so untrue. Honesty, it's hardly ever heard, but it's mostly what I need from you." It's ironic, isn't it? People long for honesty, and yet our world seems to be growing more dishonest, not less.

Would you say that you're an honest person? How do you measure honesty? Are you an honest person if you tell the truth more than 50 percent of the time? How about 75 percent or 90 percent? The true measure of honesty isn't in how often you tell the truth but when you tell the truth. Most people tell the truth most of the time. There's no reason not to. You'd have to be a pathological liar to lie all the time for no reason. The true test of honesty comes in whether you tell the truth even when it's hard, even when it might cost you.

Psalm 15:4 says that a truly honest person "swears to his own hurt and does not change." In other words, his word is always as good as if he'd been sworn under oath to tell the truth, and he will tell the truth even if being honest causes him to suffer. His honesty does not change with the circumstances. He doesn't back down from the truth regardless of the outcome.

You see, anybody can tell the truth when the truth has no consequences. The true test of honesty is whether we can tell the whole truth even when the consequences may be painful. Even when telling the truth means we have to confess a sin that will get us in trouble. Even when telling the truth means taking a stand on an issue that will cause you to be ridiculed or even hated. Even when telling the truth by sharing the gospel with an unsaved friend might not be received well and damage the relationship. Patience demands that we be men and women of truth no matter what the consequences.

As the old saying goes, "Good things come to those who wait"; but in order for that to always be true, we must add the phrase "on the Lord." "Good things come to those who wait on the Lord." No matter how hard life gets, no matter how messed up the world becomes, no matter how long it takes, we can rest patiently in the knowledge that God is in control. He knows what He's doing.

> Wait for the Lord; Be strong and let your heart take courage; Yes, wait for the Lord. (Psalm 27:14)

I PRAYED

(JAMES 5:13–20)

Having just written to you about patience, I must confess that I have struggled with a lack of patience most of my life, especially while driving. Many years ago while traveling to visit my parents, my daughter, Christy, who was three to four years old at the time, got carsick and threw up all over herself, the back seat, and the floor. It was a mess! Looking back, it shames me to say that between the very unpleasant smell in the car and falling behind in my "all-important" schedule to clean things up, I got mad—mad and impatient enough to chew out my daughter, make her cry and feel worse than the poor kid already did, and snap at my wife when she tried to intercede.

Being angry and trying to make up for lost time, I got a bit heavy on the gas pedal, and sure enough, it wasn't long before a state trooper raced up behind the car and pulled me over for speeding. I should have seen it as much-needed discipline from God, but instead, I foolishly complained that it was my daughter's fault for putting me in this situation in the first place; and now I was sure to get a ticket.

To my surprise, the trooper was very kind and understanding. After hearing of our troubles, he decided to let me off with a warning and said, "You have a beautiful family, so slow down and keep them safe."

As he walked back to his car, I rolled my window up while making some comment about how I couldn't believe I didn't get a ticket, and Christy, who had been very quiet because she knew I was mad at her, sheepishly said, "I prayed." I don't think that in my entire life anything has melted my heart and made me feel more ashamed of my behavior than those two words from my precious little girl. I was an angry, thoughtless dad, thoughtless of my daughter's feelings and thoughtless to seek God in prayer; but as just a little child, my daughter's first thought was to lovingly ask God that her dad not get a ticket. Jesus was certainly right when He said of His heavenly Father, "Out of the mouth of infants and nursing babies You have prepared praise for Yourself" (Matthew 21:16).

It's no coincidence that God's final word to us in James is to pray. As a matter of fact, He uses the word seven times in the last eight verses, which leaves little room for doubt that He is strongly emphasizing that coming to Him in prayer is one of our most critical supports in any and every circumstance of life. The first circumstance mentioned is suffering. This one comes pretty easy to us. It's our natural response to run to God when we need something. All of us tend to pray more often and with more urgency in suffering and trials and need, and that's good. God wants us to "cast our every care upon Him, because He cares for us" (1 Peter 5:7).

The greater challenge is to also remain diligent in prayer in joyful circumstances. Do we pour out our hearts in prayer to thank God and sing His praises for his blessings as fervently as we pour out our souls to plead for His help in times of trouble? He gives us so much more than we deserve, and to not sing His praises is to take God for granted and even take advantage of His grace. When life seems in order and things are great, rather than pray less often or less fervently, and maybe even forget to pray altogether, we need to sing God's praises all the more.

Sickness is another circumstance where we are encouraged to pray. The word *sick* doesn't refer to a cold or any other routine type of illness we all just endure and continue to function through. It refers to a debilitating kind of illness serious enough to lay us up in bed and even be life-threatening, hence the need for others to "pray over" the sick person for the Lord to "raise him up."

Therefore, in illness, we should not just pray ourselves but also ask others to pray for us. James speaks here of asking the elders of the church, and primarily, he is referring to those who hold a special office and are recognized as leaders of the church—a pastor, elders, or a deacon.

However, it's not so much because of the leadership position they hold but the strength of faith and righteousness they possess that made them qualified to hold that office in the first place. Notice that it isn't because they are an "elder" that their prayers are effective, but that it's a prayer offered in faith (verse 15) from a righteous man (verse 16); so it's not holding an office in the church that makes a person's prayer powerful but the faith they have in God and the righteousness of Jesus Christ they live by that makes their prayers effective to accomplish much.

So the point is, elders don't have an exclusive right to pray for the sick. As a pastor and Navy chaplain, I am honored to answer any request to pray for someone in a time of serious illness. However, we can ask anyone who is a person of faith in Jesus Christ and has a testimony of righteousness to pray for us. Every believer, as Hebrews 4:16 says, has the God-given right to draw near with confidence to the throne of grace so that we may receive mercy and find grace to help in time of need, not just for our needs but also for others.

What about this idea of anointing the sick with oil? Some interpret the use of oil in a sacramental sense, that this is some kind of special "holy oil" that has the power to heal the sick, but this is unlikely for three reasons. First, the Greek word used for anointing is not the word usually used for sacramental- or ritualistic-type anointing, like anointing someone as king or as a priest. The word used here is the more common Greek word for anointing that literally means to rub or smear. It was the word used to refer to the application of oil for more practical purposes like as a perfume or ointment or lotion.

The use of oils as medicine in biblical times is well documented. Greek literature of the first-century AD describes the use of oil as "the best of all remedies." Used along with wine, it was the primary medicine of the time. In the Lord's story of the Good Samaritan, Jesus says in Luke 10:34 that the Samaritan cared for the wounded man by bandaging the wounds and pouring oil and wine on them. Some have argued that if oil is just medicine, then why call the elders? Why not call a doctor? Well, there weren't that many doctors, and only the wealthy could afford them. People did their own doctoring back then as best they could. Which leads us to the third reason why oil is meant here as medicine.

Oil is mentioned as secondary to prayer. The grammar of the sentence proves it. Prayer is the main verb of the sentence, and oil is merely a participle that is subordinate to the act of prayer. The elders were called to pray. That was their primary purpose. God heals in answer to prayer, not in answer to oil. Applying a little oil as the typical homemade remedy of the time just made added sense and, by way of application, teaches us two important principles for dealing with sickness.

When we get seriously ill, what do we normally do first? We call the doctor. We have it backward. Our first response should be to pray. Even as we call 911 in an emergency, we should be praying as we push the buttons on our phone. God is the great physician! He is the source of all healing. He should be first on our minds and first among all first responders to call. Amen! But by all means, call the doctor too. The Bible doesn't support the notion that we should forsake all medicine and medical treatment to rely solely on faith to be healed, and if you're not healed then, "Gosh, that's just too bad. I guess you didn't have enough faith."

We have physical bodies that have physical needs. Do we rely on faith alone to be fed or clothed? If a person is hungry or naked, do we say, "Oh, I guess they didn't have enough faith for God to feed and clothe them?" No, God has ordained that we use our human resources to help meet the human needs around us, whether the need be food, clothing, or medical aid. Pastor George Buttrick rightly said, "Prayer is not a substitute for work, thinking, watching, suffering, or giving; it is a support for all other efforts." In other words, by all means, pray, pray fervently; but rally every other resource available as well because God uses miracles sparingly but often uses human hands to do His work. Prayer is a support in any and every circumstance.

Finally, prayer requires an attitude of surrender. "Therefore, confess your sins to one another, and pray for one another." Not all trouble or sickness is the result of sin, but it can be at times. Much like our parents had to discipline us to teach us right from wrong, our loving heavenly Father does as well (read Hebrews 12:4–11). Therefore, when we pray, we should pray with an attitude of surrender, to be willing to surrender our will to God's will, to surrender our pride and humbly confess our sins to God, to those our sins may have wronged, and to those we ask to pray for us.

Our first impulse in trouble and illness is to pray for the trouble to go away or for the sickness to be healed. But if our suffering is God's loving discipline for some rebellious sin in our lives, then praying for it to go away would be counter to God's purpose for our pain. The only way to make it go away is to confess the sin that brought on the discipline in the first place. Just praying for healing won't work, but praying to confess the sin that caused our pain will bring healing.

Now the question must be asked: how will I know if my trouble or illness is the result of a sin I must confess or for some other reason? The answer is, you will just know. God will be sure to reveal it to you by some means. Why do I say that? As a loving parent, would you ever discipline your child without telling them why, just send them to bed without supper for no good reason? Of course not, and neither would God do that to us. Discipline has no purpose unless we know why we're being disciplined. Sin has consequences! Yes, it may seem fun to us at first, but it always eventually brings trouble, heartache, and even sickness; so God's discipline will be obvious, and its painful consequences will not be removed until we pray to acknowledge our sin, repent of the wrong we've done, and ask for God's forgiveness and healing.

> Rejoice always; pray without ceasing; in everything give thanks; for this is God's will for you in Christ Jesus. (1 Thessalonians 5:16–18)

FINAL THOUGHTS

Well, it's been quite a road trip for me, and I pray it has been for you as well. I must say that reflecting on my driving experiences while working through the Epistle of James has helped me see my faults more clearly and heightened my awareness of just how much I need to depend on the leading of the Holy Spirit to crucify my flesh with its passions and desires (Galatians 5:24). Perhaps I should subtitle this book "Things I've Learned about Faith from behind the Wheel."

When it comes to spiritual maturity, I'm far from the "super saint" category, but God has been working to conform me to the image of Christ for over a half century; and by His grace, I have seen progress. I do pretty well controlling my temper, resisting temptations, and dealing with problems in my family or at work; but get me behind the wheel and I seem to lose all patience. Ironically, not only has writing this book deepened my faith, but I think it's making me a better driver. I've passed a lot of mile markers of faith and still have many more to go, but I'm pleased to say that I'm finally beginning to find it easier to slow down and be more patient and courteous toward others on the road.

I suspect that for many Christians in this hurry-up, hustle-and-bustle world, driving is one of the places where our faith is most tested. I have witnessed many a driver cuss out others, make crude gestures, cut people off, or speed by while proudly displaying bumper stickers that say things like "Honk if you love Jesus" or "God is not dead, I talked to Him this morning." It saddens me to think of the damage they do to the name of Christ by their less-than-Christian behavior behind the wheel. I am grateful that though I have had similar struggles, I at least have never displayed any bumper stickers that drag the name of Christ down with me.

Whether driving a car, laboring at work, relaxing at home, or worshipping in church, our faith in Christ should be an obvious reflection of His love and character; wherever we are and whomever we are with should make no difference. There is no division of life between those activities that are sacred and those that are secular. God's Word says that "whatever is not from faith is sin" (Romans 14:23). Therefore, our faith must necessarily inform and impact everything we do.

Yes, we will still occasionally fail and fall short, but praise God that our faith will not fail because God never fails. By the grace He has so abundantly poured out on us and into us, through Jesus Christ, we have the promise of His eternal love and protection. As Jude, the brother of James, was inspired to write,

> Now to Him who is able to keep you from stumbling, and to make you stand in the presence of His glory blameless with great joy, to the only God our Savior, through Jesus Christ our Lord, be glory, majesty, dominion and authority, before all time and now and forever. Amen. (Jude 24–25)

ABOUT THE AUTHOR

David Slater is an ordained minister with fifteen years' experience as a church pastor. He holds a Master of Divinity degree from Grace Theological Seminary. He is also a retired Navy chaplain with twenty-two years of military service to include a total of five combat tours in Iraq, Afghanistan, and the Persian Gulf. A gifted preacher, he has a unique ability to teach God's Word in a very simple, direct, and clear manner and show its relevance to everyday life. Happily married for over forty years, he resides with his wife, Tracie, in Springville, California. They have two adult children and one grandchild.